HORSE SENSE

HORSE SENSE

LAPO MELZI

This edition March 2023

ISBN: 88-907154-4-8

ISBN-13: 978-88-907154-4-0

On the cover: Filippo Bossetti, Notturno di Valmarina, Alessandro Dentis, Daniele Riccardi, Vincenzo Consiglio

TABLE OF CONTENTS

1

JAMIE & ACORN

It was one of the first warm days of spring at the Blackshears' farmstead. It had been a long and dreary winter this year and, for a while, it seemed like the sun would keep on hiding forever behind the clouds. When it finally started shining again, the woods around the property erupted with a green so lush it almost hurt the eyes.

Now, the walls of the old house gleamed ocher in the late afternoon light, cut against the bright green that embraced them on either side.

Winter had left its mark on the old facade, wedging in some more cracks and peeling off the paint at the edges. The once-beautiful wrought iron balcony balustrade hung bare. The dark wood panels that adorned its many frames had rotted away a few years ago and rust boils had blossomed all through the length of the opaque dark metal.

In contrast, the roof of bright corrugated aluminum sheets covering the stables gleamed in the sunlight, stained only by the remains of autumn leaves gathered in brown heaps along its length and in the gutters.

Obstacles lay scattered in the same way down in the large

gray sand school that spread in front of the house. The repetitive hits of horses' hooves had scarred many of the rails, shaving the paint down to the raw wood. Like tree rings, the bared layers of color now mercilessly showed the age of each pole.

Everything lay silent under the afternoon sun. Even the shelters of the farm animals looked deserted. The only thing moving nearby was a horse.

His name was Acorn, a handsome five-year-old appaloosa, curious and intelligent. His coat was a deep and shaded bay with a bright-white dotted blanket over his hips and buttocks. His wet, dark eyes were searching the place, eagerly but cautiously looking for something or someone.

His hooves clip-clopped on the concrete pavement in front of the stables. The other horses stared at him with a mix of envy and curiosity. Apparently, only Acorn had been granted the luxury of walking around on his own. Many of the older horses didn't seem too pleased by such blatant favoritism toward the youngster. Others, maybe more lenient or less unhappy about spending most of their time in a box, looked like they had made peace with such state of affairs and were just asking themselves what was going on.

Sandwiched between the stables and two wooden sheds, Acorn advanced warily. The rickety structures on his right bore the signs of a hasty construction and stood crooked on the bare earth. A think skeleton of iron reddened by rust held them up, while wood planks of uneven lengths came together to form approximate walls.

Through the many slits between the planks of the first shed, Acorn made out dark, vague shapes. His ears twitched as he listened intently, but he only heard the whispers of straw shifting and the sighs of sheep dozing off. A few feet farther, he stretched his ears again. From the second shed resounded a wet, spooky snort. Acorn shied away as he recognized the presence of Brunga, the Blackshears' dangerously unpredictable bull.

In his preoccupation to get as far away as possible from him, Acorn didn't realize he had stepped within bite's length of the other horses. Melinda, an old, white mare, bared her teeth and snapped at him. Acorn wriggled away just in time. He glowered at her, pulled his ears back and slid away.

Meanwhile, the object of Acorn's search was running stealthily toward a drinking trough in the paddock. His name was Jamie and he was the only son of the Blackshears—a skinny, bright eleven-year-old with restless green eyes. As he ran at the top of his lungs, the patch on his faded jeans flapped in the wind and his shapeless T-shirt rippled like a sail. His clothes looked well past their prime and not exactly his size. They were in fact hand-me-downs from his better-off cousins, but he didn't care, because his true joys were the outdoors and animals. One animal in particular was dear to him above all others: his horse Acorn—the very bay horse who was now intently looking for him, unaware of what he was scheming.

Jamie had just had a marvelous idea for a prank against Acorn that required skill and daring and he was beside himself to make it happen as soon as possible. Ten minutes before, when his brain had positively exploded with delight, he had been behind the house climbing a tree while Acorn watched him perplexed or possibly envious. On a hunch, he had plunged his hand in his pocket and got hold of his Menthos. Since Acorn loved them, he had immediately scattered a handful onto the ground as a diversion. Right after Acorn had lunged for them, he had jumped down and sneaked away, heading like a thunderbolt toward the paddock.

Now it was time to do justice to his brilliant idea. He reached the edge of the paddock and stopped in front of a trough filled with water and dead leaves that lay in the shade of tall black locust trees.

He cast a quick glance back and his wild, ash-brown hair swung back with him. Seeing Acorn hadn't spotted him, he sat down on the brim of the trough. He hesitated a second, then he propped himself up and sank his feet into the water. A chilling stream gushed through the holes in his shoes' soles and soaked his socks almost instantly. Goose bumps ran from his legs all the way up to his arms and he shivered, breathing quickly—it was just May after all and the trough stood all day in the shade. There was no time to waste on second thoughts. Jamie willed himself to withstand the cold and slowly lowered his body into the trough. He winced as the chilly water licked the whole length of his back, shooting prickling shivers up to his ears, but he didn't make any sudden movement. He didn't want to spill any water and give away his whereabouts. His heart was beating fast. It was awesome!

He took two big breaths, pinched his nose shut between his fingers and sank his head underwater, then he pressed his feet and hands against the inner walls of the trough to keep himself from floating up. Inside this shell of wood and water, the calm was eerie, even if the cold was so intense that it felt like entombing yourself in ice. Nevertheless, Jamie felt his mind relax—it was cozy in there. He pondered that perhaps that's how Acorn had felt in his mom's belly—apart from the cold, of course. Above him, through the settling water, the tree branches swayed dreamily in the breeze. Cast against the bright sky, they looked like giant feelers carefully searching the air.

Jamie stretched his ears, listening for any signs of Acorn approaching. Holding his breath underwater, still as a statue, he looked like a weird submarine stick-bug ready to pounce. His ash-brown hair fanned out around his face like wild thoughts, while his grass-green eyes gleamed with anticipation. His hiding spot was perfect! Acorn would never think of that. He really wanted to burst into an evil chuckle, but kept himself in check—he didn't want to blow his cover.

A sliver of froth drifted lazily on the surface of the water. Jamie wondered whether it was Acorn's saliva or the sheep's and he realized that he was probably lying in a tub of spit. He grinned, thinking himself daring, even though he knew that most kids at school would likely consider him disgusting. Well, who cared what they thought; they didn't know anything about adventure. Spit you just washed away, but adventure staid for the rest of your life!

A constricting sensation, as of a belt tightening steadily around his chest, made his head lighter. His lungs started screaming for air, but he was resolved to stay put. He fidgeted at the bottom of the trough, worried that Acorn wouldn't show up. Where the heck was that knucklehead? What if he didn't turn up and ruined his awesome ambush?

A wave of fretting panic seized him. Maybe he should have left a string of Menthos leading to the trough. Man! That's exactly what he should have done! Why hadn't he thought about that before? Why would Acorn come straight into the paddock? He could easily walk into the school instead. He hadn't planned this thing properly—that was going to be his downfall!

Dark thoughts of failure clouded his brain as the air in his lungs quickly expired. He reckoned he had no more than a dozen seconds left in him, then he'd have to take a breath or die in his watery tomb. Another five seconds elapsed. It was over…

Presently, a shadow draped across the trough. The temperature dropped a couple of degrees. Jamie wondered how on Earth he could feel colder than he already was, but apparently he could. The shadow moved in a little closer. He saw the darkness break up at the fringes, drawing the rough outline of a mane. Excitement fired through his skin—Acorn had come at last! He let go of his supports and kicked hard toward the surface.

He exploded out of the water in a huge splash, flailing his arms like a madman, roaring, "Raaaaugh!!"

Acorn shied back, flaring his nostrils in shock.

"Got you! I got you!" Jamie taunted. "Spoooky!"

Acorn bared his teeth and snapped at him, outraged.

Jamie plunged his hand into the frigid water and splashed him treacherously.

Acorn let out a grunt and bucked away, kicking and neighing. He shook his head around to show his disapproval for the scandalous treatment.

Jamie watched him with satisfaction, overjoyed by the result of his ambush. Best! Prank! Ever! He jumped out of the trough and romped around the paddock.

With his tail high, Acorn trotted about jerkily, wheeling his head in quick bursts, flaring his nostrils noisily at anything he laid his eyes on, as if purposefully looking for something else to get scared by. It seemed like he was actually enjoying the rush of adrenaline running wild in his veins. Jamie ran beside him, roaring and laughing, his sneakers squeaking and sloshing loudly.

At the ruckus, a few sheep poked their heads out of their shed, while the horses in the stables pricked up their ears, wondering what it was all about.

Acorn and Jamie romped around for a few more minutes, then another mischievous idea lit up Jamie's brain like a firecracker. He stopped dead in his tracks and raised his hand, splashing and dripping water everywhere.

Acorn raised his ears to full attention, an expectant expression widening his crazed eyes.

"To the pen!" Jamie shouted triumphantly.

Acorn knew that command very well. He bucked his

approval and rushed forward out of the paddock.

As they ran, Jamie remembered how Acorn, since he was a yearling, had displayed that strong shepherding instinct that cutting horses and shepherd dogs have. From then on, one of his favorite pastimes had been to break into the sheep pen and see how long he could hold one away from the rest. Acorn loved it and he loved watching him. And he could have sworn that even the sheep had warmed to it, because they got better at every round. He liked to picture them in the barn at night keeping score and bragging about their latest moves.

It was not clear whether the sheep agreed with Jamie or not, but they all quickly cowered inside as the pair of rogues skidded to a halt in front of their shelter.

In the stall nearby, Brunga snorted and turned around. Underneath his broken horn, his bloodshot eye gleamed with malice toward the intruders.

Acorn and Jamie flinched and quickly shuffled forward.

Jamie got hold of the swiveling fences attached to the sheep's pen and pulled them to the shed. He fastened them to their latches, creating a corridor between the shed and the pen. Then he jumped inside the shed, opened the gate and drove the sheep out as they bleated in confusion.

Acorn watched the woolly animals filing in front of him, his eyes flashing from one to the other as if counting.

The sheep shot inside the pen and gathered in a heap at the farthest corner.

Jamie unlatched the fence and Acorn stormed in. The sheep broke ranks and hurtled in every direction. Acorn pulled back his ears, bared his teeth and with a couple of well-placed lunges gathered them back together.

Jamie climbed onto the fence to get a better view.

Acorn surveyed the herd coolly, his wet, dark eyes searching through the mass of woolly creatures. He apparently found what he was looking for and aimed ahead.

Jamie followed his gaze and landed on Pillow, a fluffy ram that was studying Acorn with apprehension. Despite the name and the appearance, Pillow was one of the most athletic sheep in the herd, and one of the shrewdest ones. More than once, he had proved a worthy challenge for Acorn.

"Good choice, buddy!" Jamie called out.

Acorn twitched his ears, but did not look away from the sheep. He studied the herd for one more second, then bolted forward, cutting through them decisively. The sheep broke ranks again. This time, Acorn let them trickle away and zeroed in on Pillow. He spread his forelegs wide, dropped his head low until his nose skimmed the dust on the ground, and crouched down in an almost feline chasing pose. He looked like a hunting animal ready to pounce or a runner ready to sprint from the blocks.

Cornered, Pillow broke out in a frenzy.

Acorn, gathered up underneath himself and perfectly balanced, responded lightning fast to Pillow's erratic jolts. His huge body seemed to glide in the air despite its impressive mass. Like a defensive basketball player, he marked Pillow closely, anticipating his every move and sealing any escape route. With his head low and his eyes locked on him, he pressed closer, pushing Pillow's and his own reflexes to the limit.

Jamie watched mesmerized. Acorn's muscles gleamed in the late afternoon light; Pillow's coat billowed and swayed with his every move; their hooves thundered, scraped and slid on the ground. It was a superb match, all shrouded in a mystic cloud of dust that glittered against the sun. The speed and reflexes of both animals were almost blinding.

Suddenly, Acorn pulled back to take a breath. Pillow

retreated, relieved. The two went to their corners, studying each other.

With his back against the fence, Pillow darted his eyes around, taking in the whole pen, looking for a chink in Acorn's defenses. It seemed he couldn't find one. He stared at the other sheep huddled behind Acorn.

Jamie could tell that the herd instinct was building inside him. Away from his mates, he felt weak, alone, vulnerable. In a matter of seconds, he was going to break.

Acorn was watching him closely too, catching his breath.

Jamie counted under his breath. "Three... Two... One..."

Acorn nudged forward.

As if a spark had ignited under his hooves, Pillow jolted, thrusting himself at Acorn's left. Acorn pulled back almost instantly. He coiled himself up, then lunged, baring his teeth. Pillow stopped cold, then wheeled around blindly. He threw himself back in an attempt to outrun Acorn in the other direction, but misjudged and crashed against the pen. One of the rickety bars of the fence gave way under his weight. The rusty nail popped out of the rotten wood like a cork from the bottle. A gap suddenly opened in front of Pillow. He seized his chance and squeezed himself through, running for his life.

"Hey!" Jamie cried out.

In response, Pillow bleated loudly and bolted into the open. It wasn't clear whether he was bleating in terror or triumph, but he was certainly making a magnificent escape.

Jamie meant to be angry, but he couldn't keep an admiring smile from spreading on his face. Man, that sheep was good!

Acorn was not as pleased. Snorting angrily, he galloped up to Jamie, demanding he open the gate. The sheep around him scattered, noticed the gap in the pen, then started filing out into the open.

Jamie jumped off the fence and unlatched it. Acorn bolted

past him in hot pursuit. "Wait up!" he shouted and sprinted after him, his soaked shoes squeaking as he ran at the top of his lungs.

In a second, they flashed around the corner of the house and stormed into the yard. Jamie had a faint impression of the herd of sheep parting like the Red Sea before two human figures, and then he recognized his mom with Mrs. Roeg. Too late.

"Jamie!" yelled his mother through the stampede.

He and Acorn froze in the face of authority.

Authority, as personified by Maddie Blackshear, looked rather diminutive, yet quite intimidating nonetheless. Even though she was shorter than her son, she managed to stare down at Jamie. Her black eyes gleamed with threat, crowned by a mane of wild, curly black hair that resembled her son's, but looked even more untamable. As if charged with electricity, those locks curled in the air and gave her the uncanny resemblance to the fabled monster Medusa.

"I didn't do it," Jamie blurted. "Acorn did it; I swear!"

Maddie raised her black brows in utter disbelief as she glanced at the walking skeins of wool straggling through her garden.

Acorn's gaze drifted to Pillow, now grazing happily around blue and violet tulips.

"Don't you even think of that!" Maddie yelled, raising the sleeves of her jacket to reinforce her message.

Acorn startled and looked away.

Maddie raised her finger, pointing at her son and his accomplice. "You two stay away from the sheep before I throw you both in Brunga's stall!"

That was Mom's standard threat. Never put into effect, yet still pretty effective. Brunga wasn't known for his good manners —he had broken a couple of Dad's ribs once and Mom's wrist another, so a trip to his stall would probably entail some kind of physical damage.

Mrs. Roeg giggled, amused.

Jamie turned to her, exploiting the chance to take immediate evasive action. Mrs. Roeg was one of Mom's few friends and he liked her. She was a willowy, auburn-haired woman with lady-like manners. Whenever he looked at her, he couldn't help thinking of honey—maybe it was the gold tone of her skin or her warm smile that did it. He didn't know, but he found her very pleasant and pretty. He smiled politely at her. "Hello, Mrs. Roeg."

"Hello, dear," she replied, beaming, then she turned to Maddie and winked. "Looks like Captain Chaos and Helper are on a new mission."

Maddie glared at her son's drenched clothes and shook her head.

Jamie made to open his mouth and explain.

Maddie waved her hand impatiently. "I don't even want to know."

Jamie grinned. He was going to tell her later anyway. He was sure Mom would find his adventure very amusing. She usually liked it when he came up with wild plans. He hoped he could at least get a laugh out of her—it was always a treat to see Mom laugh.

He turned expectantly to Mrs. Roeg. If she was here, then maybe... "Did Holly come?" he asked in one breath.

Mrs. Roeg's eyes shifted; something like a shadow passed over her smile. "No, she had to stay home. She said she was behind in math."

Jamie's grin died away. Of course, he thought.

Mrs. Roeg threw him a strange glance. "Sorry, dear."

Jamie shrugged. These days, Holly didn't come to visit him anymore. It sucked. He didn't understand why she always had to be so busy. He was mulling over these thoughts when he felt his mom's hand running through his hair. The touch of her skin made him feel a little better.

"Dry out your clothes," Maddie said gently, "or you'll catch a cold."

Jamie nodded.

She bent down and gave him a kiss.

Jamie felt the warmth from her lips spread to his chest. Oh well, perhaps Holly was really busy after all. He'd ask her to come play with him and Acorn next time. "Good-bye, Mrs. Roeg!" he said, turning to her.

She beamed, apparently relieved he was in good mood again. "Good-bye, Captain!"

Jamie's smile flashed back on his lips. He saluted militarily and ran off with Acorn.

"Jamie," Maddie yelled after him, "get those sheep back into the shed!"

Flustered, Jamie stopped in his tracks. "Oh, right, right!"

2

NOT WELCOME

Jamie woke up with a start and looked around, trying to get his bearings. He felt something bright brushing the side of his face. He turned and saw a shaft of yellow light cut across his body, then he recognized his bed, his room and the beam of the streetlamp that stood next to the house. He closed his eyes and let the glare seep through his eyelids. The sense of time flowed back into him. He opened his eyes. It was morning, Monday morning. Your next paragraph goes here.

Again, he thought. It should have gotten used to it by now, but waking up with a start every other day always took him by surprise.

The alarm clock went off—it was 5:45 AM.

He stretched out his arm and switched it off. Once again he wondered what jolted him awake like that; why it happened. A vague sense of uneasiness and anxiety hung to him. He knew the only way to get rid of it was to move, so he tossed the blanket aside and stepped out of bed.

The cold air of his bedroom slapped him fully awake. He slipped into his working clothes and marched downstairs. He never liked the sensation of wearing something over dirty skin, but it was pointless to clean himself before doing his chores. He was going to take a shower and brush his teeth after he finished. As he was descending the stairs, he suddenly realized his muscles hurt. He felt cold and rigid. The fact that the heat in the house was off did not help the situation. As soon as he got into the kitchen, he grabbed his jacket from the wall hanger and put it on.

Maddie greeted him with a kiss. "Good morning, tiger."

"Morning, Mom!"

She smiled and brought a mug of steaming hot milk over to him. "Did you sleep well?"

"Yeah," Jamie lied.

"You're cold?"

"Just a bit," he said in a croaky voice.

"Hmm..." She frowned, but did not elaborate.

Jamie flicked on an evasive smile and sat down.

She went back to the kitchen counter to get his breakfast.

He knew what she wanted to say: he probably shouldn't have gotten himself soaked at the beginning of May. True, but he didn't regret an instant of it. He was happy to deal with a cold if it came down to it, in exchange for the great moment he had enjoyed. Maybe Mom could tell what he was thinking, because she didn't say anything. Or perhaps she shared the same appreciation for adventure he had—she did like to hear the recounts of his deeds, after all. Whatever the reason, she didn't argue and he was thankful. It always felt like she was on his side, that she understood him.

He shivered and hugged the jacket tighter. What he would also have really appreciated was if they had more money and could afford turning on the heat more often. He hated having breakfast in the cold. The worst was feeling the freezing air seep through his clothes when he lifted his arms to take a bite. Because of that, he always ended up eating too fast without realizing it. Every time, he would find himself with a tight, heavy knot in his stomach, colder than when he had started and completely unsatisfied. It totally spoiled the pleasure of the first meal of the day.

Maddie came back with a plate of bread and butter sprinkled with sugar. "Enjoy. I'll finish feeding the horses."

"I'll be there in a sec too."

She kissed his forehead and threw on a jacket.

He watched her walking out of the door and thought that he really didn't envy her. Every morning, Mom woke up early and started doing heavy work right from the start, while Dad slept in. A pang of anger hit Jamie. Sure his father drove around as a horse feed salesman and taught at the riding school, but he left all of the physical hard labor to Mom. That wasn't fair. She was strong, but all that work was too much even for a man. She shouldn't be treated that way—she was nice—she should have time to enjoy herself. Instead, all she did was work like a slave. If only they could be rich... Jamie snorted. Sure, as if wishing would change anything. He glanced at the wall clock—it was already 6:05 AM. He had better get going.

He drank the milk slowly, fighting the urge to gulp down the whole mug at once, and methodically chewed the first slice of bread and butter, then stood up. He zipped up his jacket, grabbed the other slice, then went out of the kitchen and into the cold air of the May morning. Chewing, he walked into the feed room, filled a measuring cup and walked out.

As he entered the stables, he was welcomed by the barky smell of wood shavings mixed with the grassy tang of hay. There was also a more subdued, warm scent in the air: that of horses' skin. He liked that scent a lot, because it was more than a simple smell to him. It was a rippling in the air that carried the warmth of the horses' bodies, that flexed with their huge muscles and beat together with their big, generous hearts. Through that, he could feel their presence even if he couldn't see them. It was their ghost: a shadow that seeped into your clothes, your hair, your own skin—a reminder of them that you carried with you everywhere you went.

As he drew closer, other less pleasant smells emerged. The acrid stink of urine was the more pungent one and it only punctuated some of the boxes where the horses had obviously relieved themselves. Then there was the far less offensive odor of their droppings, which still held a distinctive scent of hay and grass. Jamie thought that compared to human poop it smelled like flowers. There was no doubt in his mind that if even their poop smelled good these must be really nice animals. That was another reason why it didn't bother him at all to take care of them.

As he passed through the hallway, he glanced at the box nearby and spotted his mom with Dillinger, his dad's favorite horse. She finished pouring some feed into his manger, then bent down and petted Milly, Dillinger's companion Tibetan goat. Dillinger was pretty neurotic, so he needed the company of his little horned friend to relax.

Jamie pushed the big metal doors of the stables open and walked outside, toward Acorn's box. He spotted the wheelbarrow and fork set next to the door. He smiled—Mom had already brought them there for him. "Thanks!" he shouted, turning back.

"You're welcome, babe!"

He opened the box. Acorn blinked and let out a welcoming nicker. Jamie smiled. "Morning, buddy." He poured the feed in the manger, checked that the nose paddle in the drinking bowl was clean of muck and worked freely, then turned around. A chuckle escaped his lips at the sight of Acorn's sleepy expression: his lower lip hung limply from his mouth; his blurry eyes still stuck with sleep stared blankly at him; and his forelock stood askew over his forehead, plastered in wood shavings.

"Here." He stepped up and started brushing his tuft with his fingers. Acorn turned away, too morning-grumpy to stand any grooming. "Come on, you're a mess!" Jamie seized his head and kept him still. Acorn let out a groan, but didn't fight back. "Done. Come here." He slipped under his neck and hugged him, resting his cheek against his warm skin. He closed his eyes and so did Acorn. They both dozed off for a few seconds, then Jamie patted him and pulled away. "Back to work now!"

He dragged the wheelbarrow to the door, got hold of the fork and started cleaning the box in earnest. This wasn't really a chore for him. He took pride in caring for Acorn—it was an act of respect and love toward his friend to make sure he lived and slept in a clean place.

After twenty minutes, he was all sweaty, but done. He patted Acorn goodbye and hurried to see to his other chores.

As Mom finished cleaning the sheep shelter and Brunga's stall, he went back to the feed room. He took well measured slices from the hay bales and distributed them among the horses. Next, he helped her feed the sheep, checked that all the drinking bowls in the stables worked, and then he was done.

The sky started to clear, kindled by the sun rising behind the hills. Jamie checked his watch: it was 7:10 AM.

"It's going to be a nice day," Maddie said cheerily. "Get in the shower and I'll drive you to school."

"I'd rather bike."

She raised her brow. "Isn't it too cold?"

Jamie smiled. "No, it's fine. I'll bundle up." He knew she was worried he might be nursing a cold. It was a bit chilly in fact, but he didn't want to set foot in their old shaky car. Riding inside Thelma —that was what his mom called it—always felt like sitting on a really bad, old washing machine: everything shook so violently, you lost the sensation in your body. At a certain point, you felt like you were floating, as if you were entering another dimension. Biking to school, even in the cold, was a much better alternative.

"All right," sighed Maddie. "But cover yourself or you'll catch a cold."

"OK." Jamie nodded and took off.

After a quick shower, he jumped on his bike—a no frills four gears piece of metal inherited from his grandfather—and started his fifteen minutes ride to school.

He left the farmstead behind and passed by the Grangers' cattle farm, then by the veterinarian's clinic, puffing as he pedaled uphill. The road leveled and he headed through the long stretch of houses that became denser and denser as he approached the center of Greensboro.

All this effort, he thought as the perspiration started cooling his skin, just to get to school and sit down for six hours. What a waste! He wished he could just keep on going and bike to the lake. Oh well... At least he was going to learn something. He liked learning new things—it was exciting. He just hoped his teacher, Ms. Ambrose, wasn't in one of her foul moods.

He passed St. Mary's Children's Home and negotiated the last steep uphill climb of the trip. He caught his breath at the top, then stood on the pedals and let the bike speed down toward school. The cold air whipped his wild hair and chilled the sweat on his chest and arms. He shivered and enjoyed the thrill of the descent. The pale yellow façade of Greensboro Elementary came into view, then the big garden in front of the main entrance. He pulled on the brakes and veered toward the black gate, sped through, then slowed down in the narrow alley that lead to the rear of the school, where the bike racks were.

As he rounded the corner, he caught sight of a group of fifth-graders who surrounded a third-grader, taunting him. He noticed the red notebook held in the hand of one of the older kids. The third-grader lunged to snatch it, but the fifth-grader shoved him off and tossed notebook to one of his friends.

A surge of anger erupted in the pit of Jamie's stomach—he hated bullies. Without thinking, he got off the bike, dropped his backpack and made his way toward the gang. Three against one, he thought—cowards!

The three bullies had their backs to him, so they did not see him coming. Jamie sneaked behind them and stole the notebook. The boys rounded on him. Jamie slipped away and handed the notebook to the third-grader. The boy snatched the pad roughly from his hands and blushed. Jamie frowned, taken aback.

"Hey!" called one of the gang.

Jamie turned.

"Whaddaya think you're doing!?" the skinniest boy of the three challenged, throwing out his arms for a shove.

Jamie caught him and pushed him away. "I'm giving him back his notebook!" he said, nodding toward the third grader.

The skinny boy flashed him a nasty look. He had a ratty feeling about him: he was gaunt and twitchy, with pale chestnut hair and beady eyes.

Jamie studied the other two. One was a bull-like kid with glassy eyes and thick hands with fingers like sausages. The other was lanky, with bleary, shifty eyes.

"Is he your friend?" Ratty asked with a nasty glint in his eyes.

"No, I don't know him."

"Then mind your own business!"

"This is my business."

"Oh yeah!?" said Bull, cracking his knuckles.

"Yeah!" Jamie whipped back, turning to him. "It doesn't make any difference if I know him or not. Leave him alone!"

Bull stalked forward. "Who do you think you are, Superman!?"

Jamie instinctively stepped forward too. "I am Jamie! Who are you!?"

The boy balked, wrong-footed. He frowned, suddenly wary. "You're weird!"

Jamie grinned to make it even weirder. At that moment, he caught sight of Shifty turning around and spotting his backpack on the ground, next to his bike. Before the boy could make a run for it, Jamie lunged and shoved him off. Shifty tripped and fell. Jamie sprinted forward and grabbed his backpack. As he straightened up, he saw Holly, a few feet away, holding her bike and staring at him. He didn't have time to say hi. He wheeled around, flinging the backpack on his shoulders, ready to pick up his bike if he needed to. To his relief, the three bullies seemed too taken aback to retaliate. Bull was helping Shifty one to his feet. Behind them, the third-grader took his chance and slinked away inside the school.

Good, he thought. At least now he was out of their reach.

The three bullies turned around, ready to take out their frustration on the smaller kid, but discovered he was gone. Fuming, they muttered some imprecations and withdrew.

Jamie sighed with relief. He turned to retrieve his bike and noticed Holly was still there. "Hi!" he called out too cheerfully, the adrenaline still rushing through his body.

Holly tossed a dismissive wave at him and started pushing her bike toward the racks.

Jamie picked up his bike and stepped next to her. "Did you see that?" he asked chattily. He felt wired, overexcited, over-charged, but couldn't help himself.

"Yeah," Holly answered flatly. "You were fighting again."

He frowned. "I wasn't fighting. I was just helping that boy. They were bullying him, didn't you see?"

Holly pursed her lips. "Hmm, hmm."

Jamie stiffened. "And he didn't even say thank you. That was rude."

"Well, you were rude first!"

"What's that supposed to mean?"

"You always go around sticking your nose into other people's business, Jamie. You should wait for people to ask you for help. It's rude!"

"What!? I should wait until somebody gets beaten up before helping!? Are you crazy!?"

Holly shot him a nasty look. "I was just giving you some advice!" She turned around and strode away.

Jamie stopped in his tracks, boiling with anger and confusion. "Great," he muttered under his breath. "A really great start, this morning."

3

THE GAME

Jamie pushed hard on the pedals and sped toward home. Even hours later, Holly's words were still ringing in his ears. He spun his legs furiously, pushing until it hurt too much to go on, then sat back on his bike, out of breath, and let the momentum carry him downhill, the wind whipping his cheeks and chest.

He still felt restless, overwrought. He hoped the burning in his chest and muscles would get rid of the edge, and didn't understand why he dwelt so much on what had happened, but he couldn't help it.

At last, he arrived at home and parked his bike against the wall of the house. He noticed that Thelma wasn't in the driveway and neither was his dad's car. He walked up to the kitchen and made to pull the door open—it was locked. So they were out, he thought. He turned around, caught sight of the potted red geranium plant on the windowsill and walked up to it. He lifted the flowerpot and found the keys lying underneath. There was also a note. He picked it up and read.

Taking care of some errands. Be back in a couple.
Dad is out too.
Sandwich and some fruit in the fridge.

P.s. Don't wreck the house! ;-)

Love,
Mom

Jamie sighed. He had wanted to eat something with her. That would have calmed him down. He unlocked the door and walked in. The silence of the still house enveloped him. He felt the unpleasant restlessness inside him rear its head again. He was still hurt that Holly of all people would call him rude. She was the first real friend he had made in school. She used to come and play with him and Acorn. They had been really close.

He paused in front of the fridge—he needed to do something; he didn't want to sit in the empty house. And since he was at it, he better find something good, something worthy, a challenge maybe. He needed Acorn! He wheeled around and bolted out of the house.

Slamming the wicket gate open, he rushed to the paddock.

As he heard him approaching, Acorn turned around. He broke into a gallop and skidded to a halt in front of the exit.

"All right, buddy," Jamie called out, pulling the gate open. "You're with me?"

Acorn trotted out with eyes gleaming in anticipation.

He needed another brilliant idea, Jamie told himself, a stroke of genius that would make all his previous deeds pale in comparison. His gaze roved around the property, hungry to latch on to something.

Crushed by his own expectations, he came up empty. He

turned around and met Acorn's huge, wet eyes staring eagerly at him. He frowned, ashamed at his sudden lack of imagination. His eyes glided aimlessly over Acorn's body. A thin line of dust and sweat was stuck on his chest. His enormous ribs heaved with his every breath.

Jamie cracked a smile as inspiration finally struck. That's right, sometimes new things are just not as exciting as your favorite game! A wave of pleasure ebbed through him as he tested the idea in his mind. Yep, that was it.

"Let's do it, then!" he called out.

Acorn startled at his sudden burst of energy. He flicked up his ears to full attention.

"Ready for a game?" Jamie clapped his hands and broke into a run toward the back of the house. "Let's go!"

Acorn's eyes lit up. He bolted forward and followed suit.

In an instant, they cleared the corner of the stables and headed for a rusty basketball hoop nailed haphazardly to the back wall. On its right, resting on some protruding bricks, stood a weatherworn chalk scoreboard bearing their names in Jamie's chicken-scratch handwriting.

Acorn stopped under the hoop and waited for Jamie, obviously used to the routine.

Jamie reached into a nook between a stack of grimy unused tiles and the brick wall. A second later, he extracted a raggedy mini basketball that looked like it had stood some pretty rough handling. Its once-deep orange surface was now covered in scratches and scuffs and was as discolored and worn out as the scoreboard. Jamie cradled it in his arms as he walked back to the makeshift basketball court in front of the hoop.

"All right, Mr. A-Corn," he cried out, stopping in front of him. "Let's see if you can do better than with those sheep amateurs. Here's the real deal!"

Sensing they were going to start the game, Acorn crouched down.

Jamie made to dribble and advance, but the basketball just slapped the ground like a wet towel, its deflated body too slack to bounce properly.

Taken aback, Acorn pulled up, his ears pricked up in a questioning pose.

Jamie quickly bent down and picked up the ball, raising his hand as if to stifle any questioning. "Just a sec. We're having some technical difficulties..." He squeezed the ball between his hands to better appraise how inflated it was. "It's all good," he grunted. "We're professionals here, we can handle this." He slammed it hard on the ground and it bounced back into his hand. "There you go!" he said, dribbling forward.

Acorn's eyes locked on him. He turned his ears forward at full attention, lowered his head and spread out his forelegs for balance. The match was on.

Jamie glanced up at his intense expression and knew he was in trouble. Bouncing that saggy ball was already proving challenging enough. He needed a quick fix. "Watch the ball, man!" he started chanting like a street magician. "Watch the ball!" Suddenly, he jumped and threw in a nice arc.

Acorn raised his head with a questioning look. The mini basketball flew over him and fell with a clean swoop through the hoop.

"Yeah!" Jamie exulted, pumping his fist.

Acorn watched perplexed as the ball rolled limply on the ground. He puffed impatiently: that was not the game! He turned to Jamie, who feigned surprise and stretched his arms.

"What's going on?"

Acorn goggled at him, mystified by his behavior.

Jamie dropped the pretense and picked up the ball, grinning broadly. "Oh, yeah, I scored!"

Acorn registered the mockery and glowered at him.

"Uhh, you're giving me the death stare! Uh, Mommy, look, Acorn is giving me the death stare. Oh, I'm so scared!"

Acorn snorted hard.

Jamie, though, was too drunk with the glory of his wit to relent his taunting. "Dig it, man. Check this out!" He flicked the ball up in midair, then caught it with a twirl around. "I'm the man, the King in his court!"

Judging by the look on his face, Acorn would have probably leveled Jamie to the ground with a sarcastic retort if he could speak. Since he couldn't, he contented himself with turning away, looking bored to death.

"Hey! I saw you do that!"

Acorn turned around with an innocent blank expression on his face.

"So you wanna challenge the King!?" Jamie slapped the ball hard on the ground, getting ready for another attack.

Acorn's eyes grew covetous.

"Watch out, man! I'm so fast, I'll send you back in time and you'll lose again!" Without warning, he dashed forward.

Acorn's instinct switched on in an instant. With a smooth and powerful slide, he ducked down and lunged.

Jamie saw his huge body hurtle toward him and he back-tracked in a hurry, turning around to protect the ball. That sneak almost got him, he thought breathlessly. He had cooked him nice and slow, but that knucklehead still had the freakish reflexes of a cat!

He weighed his options. He could go for another three-pointer, but that would be like admitting he couldn't outwit that brainless bronco. No, no, he was going to win fair and square! He wheeled around and launched himself into a frenzy of feints, counterfeints, counter-counterfeints. In his mind, he was imitating the professional basketball players he had seen on TV, looking cool and smooth as he performed some amazing moves. In reality, he was flailing his limbs around madly, resembling more a possessed drunken chicken with an epileptic fit than a pro player.

One thing he was doing right, though: he looked confusing. Too bad that Acorn didn't buy it. With effortless flair, he was anticipating his every move as if he could read his mind.

Jamie couldn't stand it. He had taught Acorn; he was the master; he was the one with hands and opposable thumbs. It was ludicrous; he couldn't lose!

He pushed forward, desperate to break the siege. He groaned and moaned and sweat, but Acorn didn't relinquish any ground. He was there wherever he went, like his shadow, his eyes glistening as if stopping him was the most important thing in the universe.

Exasperated, Jamie grimaced. Nothing he tried would work. That slack ball had proven a total liability. In one last mighty effort, he pulled together all his strength and went for broke. He spun around twice to the left, feinted a shot, then threw himself to the right to catch Acorn off guard, but he lost balance and overreached.

As soon as Acorn saw the ball clean in front of him, he pulled back his ears and lunged to bite. Jamie saw his jaws spring open like the gate of hell. He let go in a hurry. Acorn's huge mouth snapped shut around the ball. His thumb-size teeth clamped the rubber and squeezed it with enormous strength, making it creak.

Jamie jumped back. Instinctively, he rubbed his fingers on his T-shirt, checking that they were still attached, and then he caught himself. Fool! Acorn had banked on his fear and he had fallen for it. Played like a sheep!

"You!" he called out indignantly, pointing a finger. "This is basketball, you mule, not murderball!"

In response, Acorn neighed at the top of his lungs, raising the prize in his mouth. He jerked his head and tail high and trotted around like the king of horses.

"Yeah, yeah, strut your stuff," grunted Jamie, but he couldn't suppress a smile. "Enjoy your small victory while you can!"

Acorn paraded around shamelessly.

"Fine, fine, you scored. Big deal! Are you going to give me back that ball, or do you want to sleep with it?" He grinned, looking at the poor basketball squeezed between Acorn's jaws. Their game wasn't for wimps. No, sir, their game was a full contact sport—Ooh, yeah!—It was their tradition, their little secret society. Mom had been briefed, of course, and sometimes she came to watch a match, but she was the only one admitted. By now he knew too well how other people would look at him: just like his father had done—as if he and Acorn were a freak show routine. He had also told a couple of his friends at school once, and they hadn't stopped laughing. People were so dumb about these things. He couldn't really wrap his head around it. Sure, he was playing basketball with a horse, but he wasn't really playing basketball. A horse can't play basketball like a human. Plus, what he was doing was pretty logical. Acorn had that shepherding instinct, so he had thought he would mark him too if he made the whole thing into a game. And so Acorn did. What was so weird about that?

Jamie shrugged and shook out of his reverie. "Come on, man, give it back. We've got to finish this game!"

Acorn pricked up his ears and studied him eagerly.

Jamie stepped forward, stretching his hand.

Acorn bolted away, bucking.

"All right, whatever! We'll make it a draw this time, OK?" He walked to the scoreboard and scratched a white stick under his and Acorn's name, then he turned around. "Happy?"

Acorn stared at him, the manic glint still flickering in his eyes.

Jamie looked at the sky. He felt much better. What he needed now was to celebrate. "Let's go!"

He ran home. Since mom was out, he didn't even try to hide his impetus for going into the house. He wrenched open the door, letting it crash against the wall. He stormed into the kitchen, ransacked Mom's private stash of sweets, grabbed a handful of multicolored candies, and rushed out slamming the door so hard that a fleck of paint came away from the wall. Mom would have killed him for that, had she been there. Jamie grinned at another mischief successfully carried out.

Acorn had finally dropped the basketball and tailed him as they ran back toward the paddock, curious to discover what they would do next.

Jamie aimed straight for his favorite spot, a patch of soft grass next to a huge, old chestnut tree. He sat down and his eyes fell on his discolored, frayed jeans. It would have been nice for once to own his own instead of having to take hand-me-downs from his cousins, he thought. Acorn's muzzle brushed his head. He looked up. Acorn's wet eyes were pointed at him with a questioning look. Jamie smiled. Clothes were just stuff after all, he thought. Who cared really. They didn't mean anything when you could have a friend like Acorn around. He leaned back, letting the sun envelop him in its golden warmth.

Acorn, still waiting for the next call to action, puzzled over Jamie's apparent lack of motivation. He didn't seem satisfied with just hanging around. He started searching for something to do, then noticed Jamie's unkempt hair and decided that would do. He stepped closer and started picking methodically at each strand with his big, fleshy lips, so as not to hurt Jamie, then, like an expert hairdresser, he twisted them as he pulled, making them stand on end.

Jamie sat still, always amused and mesmerized by this quirk. He had no idea why Acorn liked to mess with his hair so much. He didn't know if it meant affection or if it was more like a game of skill for him or, maybe, a stress reliever, much like playing with those squishy balls they sold at the supermarket. Who knew really, but it felt strangely pleasant and ticklish, so he let him do it.

Now that he was sitting in the sun, the idea of lazing about for a little while didn't seem at all bad. His mind drifted lazily. Unexpectedly, the thought of Holly crawled back to the surface. A cold, soggy knot tightened his stomach. All of a sudden, he felt lonely, even though Acorn was next to him. He felt a sudden rush of yearning for Holly's company. She used to be his best friend, but lately she kept on coming up with excuses. Homework... Yeah, right! She wasn't slow—it couldn't take her so long. Was she avoiding him? But why?

He glanced up at Acorn. "Who needs her, right?"

He stared back blankly.

"We're the kings of fun! We don't need nobody!"

He unwrapped two of the candies he had stolen and handed one to Acorn. He flicked his ears to full attention at the sight of the sugary treat, then he slowly inched forward. He picked up the candy between his huge, fleshy lips with the utmost care, then tasted it with anticipation. His big, watery eyes became all round.

Jamie snickered: he loved how surprised Acorn got whenever he let him try a new flavor. Each time he thought he could see his brain pop and fizzle with delight.

He dropped the other candy into his own mouth. A sweet cherry tide flooded his palate with a pleasant fizz. He smiled and nodded at Acorn. "I know what you mean, pal. This is a good one!"

Acorn glanced blankly at him, apparently too enthralled to manage any kind of response.

Jamie knew that he was lucky to have a friend like him. He just wished sometimes that Acorn could talk so they could share more things... But then, being friends with someone of another species was something magical and words were not that important, after all. To tell the truth, Acorn knew him better than most of his friends who could talk, and he knew him as well as he knew himself. He knew that Acorn had been afraid of storms, ever since that time he was out in the paddock and a bolt of lightning hit the woods nearby. He knew that he liked Menthos, but didn't like cotton candy. He knew that he had an ongoing feud with Dillinger, but loved Milly, his companion goat. He knew that he liked late afternoons, red-haired people and swimming in the river. And he knew that he loved him.

And yet...

All of a sudden, that strange yearning rushed back through Jamie. And it wasn't just for Holly this time. He felt a wrenching longing for more friends take hold of him. He was older now—he was supposed to have more friends. Why did they hardly ever come to visit him these days? When they were all smaller, many had been afraid of Acorn, but he had won them over and, for a while, they had all come over regularly. Holly especially liked Acorn and she would come hang out with the two of them a lot. Jamie still remembered the first time she and Acorn met. It happened during a trip to his own house in second grade.

Since his family had so many animals, his previous teacher, Ms. Haley, thought it would be educational to bring the whole class there.

At the time, Jamie had been very nervous. He was afraid of showing his classmates how poor he was, because he thought they would make fun of him. At the same time, he felt a kind of pride, because his teacher had looked very impressed when she had discovered he lived on a farm. So, he had felt alternately hot and cold, fretting and excited.

His fears were probably well placed, but what he hadn't taken into account was the fact that his classmates had never seen so many animals all at once. Soon, they had become so overwhelmed with touching, feeding and dealing with the animals, that none of them gave much notice to either the state of the house or the rusty sheep shed or the patched-up horses' boxes. There was no sniggering, no elbowing, no whispering. By the time they arrived at the paddock where Acorn was waiting for them, Jamie was in an excellent mood and ready to show off.

As they walked up to the fence, Acorn craned his neck, eager to study them more closely. Many of Jamie's classmates and Ms. Haley mistook Acorn's interest for aggressive behavior, so they fanned out around him, at a distance. Jamie walked up to Acorn, patted him and turned around. Suddenly, he found himself facing a hesitant crowd. He had pictured everybody just walking up with him and taking turns patting Acorn while he told them stories. When he saw them stalled, looking afraid, he blanked. That didn't make any sense—Acorn wasn't dangerous.

"Come on, he doesn't bite," he called out. But that made some of his classmates recoil as if they hadn't thought a horse could bite and now the prospect of getting near it was even less appealing.

Acorn twitched his ears and stiffened, disquieted by the hostile vibe.

Jamie felt him tense up under his fingers and his feet went cold with sweat. If they made him nervous, he was going to look like an idiot! It was going to be a disaster! He glanced around, desperate for anybody to come forward, when he noticed Holly in the front of the line. She didn't look scared like the others and, more importantly, her eyes were burning for Acorn. She looked like she had never seen anything more beautiful in her life.

Jamie could tell that she yearned for nothing more than to touch him, but she was too shy to make the first step. On a hunch, he raised his hand and stroked the soft bit of nose right above Acorn's upper lip where every horse feels like silk.

Acorn shifted his attention away from the crowd. Jamie's touch made him feel at ease right away. He relaxed and sighed.

"It's soft. Come touch it!" he told Holly.

Her face lit up at the offer. She stepped forward, but immediately stopped in her tracks. "Can I? Really?" she said, looking at Acorn as if asking him permission.

Acorn pricked up his ears.

"Yeah," Jamie answered. "He loves it. Come on, rub here. Feel the tiny hair and the skin."

Holly stretched out her hand.

Acorn nudged her and probed her palm with his muzzle.

Holly giggled at the tickling. Emboldened by his friendliness, she placed her hand on his nose and rubbed gently. He sighed and relaxed.

Holly turned to Jamie, delighted. "It's so soft!"

"I know." He smiled, relieved that she was into it. Now he didn't have to worry anymore.

In fact, as soon as the others saw how much Holly was enjoying herself, they all stepped up to try too. Soon Jamie was taking people in turns to pat Acorn, who in turn seemed to relish all those attentions.

Jamie shook out of his reverie. Acorn finished pulling another strand of his hair. He reached up with his hand and felt a sort of mane fanning around his head. He probably looked like a crazy scientist, he thought. He patted Acorn distractedly and was stung by a pang of melancholy about that day. All of his classmates around him... The admiration he had felt from them instead of the mockery he had expected. Why couldn't it be like that again?

Lately, it had started feeling like everybody was running away from something—he just hoped it wasn't him. A sudden chill run ran up his spine. He looked up at the sky. The sun was moving behind some clouds. The air heaved a last warm sigh, then a cold breeze glided down from the distant mountains.

4

SCHOOL

Jamie jolted awake. He struggled to recognize where he was and looked around, trying to get his bearings. Then he recognized his dirty clothes thrown on the chair, his books, his own bed, and everything started to look familiar again. The feeling in his body resurfaced too.

Again, he thought.

And this time it was worse. He felt strange, weird... What was the word? Disconcerted. Yeah, he felt disconcerted. He turned over in bed and stared at the ceiling. He rolled the word on his tongue, trying to savor its meaning, hoping it would bring him some insight. It didn't. Instead it only reinforced the uneasiness that weighed him down. There was something lurking somewhere inside him, yet he didn't know exactly what or where. He had a hunch the answer lay right beyond the wall of sleep. Something must have happened—maybe a bad dream, a nightmare. He tried to remember. Only a vague reminiscence of something unpleasant, perhaps scary, came back to him. Nothing concrete, just a blur of feeling. Jamie didn't like that at all. He didn't like being afraid of something he didn't know. He didn't like being afraid of something he knew either, for that matter, but this was worse. How could he fight what he didn't even recognize?

"Jamie, are you up!?" shouted Maddie from the ground floor.

He turned around and checked his alarm clock. It read 6:00 AM. The alarm was off. He frowned—he didn't remember waking up and switching it off.

"Breakfast is getting cold. Come down!"

"Coming! I'm coming!" He pulled back the bed sheets, threw on his working clothes and marched downstairs.

"Morning, Mom!"

"Good morning, kitten."

He noticed that the kitchen felt warmer than usual. The oven was on and gentle waves of warmth flowed toward him with a delicious fragrance of apple pie. Mom had somehow found time to bake. Now he was really looking forward to his breakfast!

Maddie handed him a generous portion of pie and put a mug of steaming hot milk in front of him. "The breakfast of champions!"

Jamie grinned. "Thanks, Mom."

Maddie smiled back, took a slice for herself and sat down at the table.

Jamie looked at her with a puzzled expression.

She winked. "I think I'll take it easy this morning."

He smiled. He liked the idea of Mom taking a break and enjoying breakfast with him.

Maddie tasted the pie, closed her eyes with pleasure and nodded proudly. "I'm goood!"

Jamie laughed. "Yeah, you are, Mom."

The sweet, woody fragrance of the pie wafted up to his nose. He inhaled and the tasty flavor warmed him, making his mouth water. He lowered his eyes and stared at his breakfast. If his mom's love could have a shape, he thought, it would be this apple pie. Well, then it would really be a sin not to eat it!

He sank his fork in the fragrant paste and took a bite. Cinnamon and apple and sugar and that brown flavor that flour has when baked to perfection, all melted in his mouth. He sighed with pleasure.

"Yep," Maddie said with a knowing grin.

He nodded. This pie was baked happiness, that's what it was! He chewed slowly, deliberately. Mom was awesome.

He reached for the mug and took a sip. As the milk poured down, his stomach gave an unpleasant throb. Weird... Well, it was early morning after all. Probably his belly just needed to warm up a little more.

He shrugged and started chipping at the pie with gusto. He sat back and let his mind wander aimlessly. He still hadn't sorted his books for the day. He was always too lazy at night and invariably forgot to prepare his backpack. He certainly didn't wish to give Ms. Ambrose any reason to be angry at him.

As he took another sip of milk, the image of Ms. Ambrose's face flashed in front of his eyes. Something stirred inside him and his stomach lurched.

He jumped up, holding his mouth for fear of spewing vomit in the kitchen. He rushed into the restroom, threw himself in front of the toilet, and let the gag reflex take over, retching violently. His stomach continued convulsing until there was nothing left inside it.

Panting, he leaned on the toilet and flushed it. He felt better now, but he also felt weaker, empty, but not just physically. There was something else, a shaking somewhere inside him. Fear? Was he scared? Of what?

He heard his mom knock at the door. "Jamie, are you OK?"

"Yeah. It's the milk."

"Are you feeling OK?"

"Just the milk. It didn't sit well with me. Don't know why."

"OK. Do you want anything else?"

"No, I'll eat something after I'm done."

"Forget about your chores today. I'll take care of it."

"No, I'm fine, really. I'll be out in a sec."

"I said don't worry, Jamie. You're off duty today, OK? You'll catch up some other time."

He sighed. He felt guilty, but he wouldn't mind taking it easy actually—he didn't feel that great. "OK. I'll just eat some bread, then."

"Good. I'll toast it, so at least you eat something warm. Come out when you're ready."

"OK."

He pulled himself up and spit the last remains of sick into the toilet. A tiny piece of apple floated on the water. What a waste, he thought. That pie had felt like such a gift. He was sure his mom would feel bad—she put so much effort into making it. He decided to take some with him to school. He wanted to show her that he really liked it and it wasn't her fault he threw up. He flushed the toilet again and walked out.

He made an effort to eat the toast, even if he still felt nauseous, then walked upstairs to take a shower and get changed.

By the time he climbed down, he was feeling much better. The nausea had almost gone away.

"Let's go. It's late," Maddie said grabbing the car keys.

Jamie wasn't looking forward to getting shaken inside Thelma, but he obediently got into their old car.

As soon as they hit the road, Thelma started rattling ominously. Jamie shifted in his seat and clutched his lunch box on his lap while he and everything around began vibrating. He wondered if that's how you felt before being beamed off by a teleporter. Now, that would have been nice instead of driving to school! Too bad good old Thelma didn't look the part of the high-tech machine. He held his breath, trying to push down the nausea that was coming back with a vengeance.

Maddie slowed down, sighting a puddle on the road.

Jamie instinctively lifted his feet. Water did not agree with Thelma. The old car had stood the abuse of many seasons and now, in its later years, it was rotting from the inside like a tree struck by a thunderbolt. Everywhere, red rust had eaten away at the metal and flaked off like the skin of an old man. Old tooth that she was, Thelma was now tunneled through with cavities: some you could see, some you could not.

He and his mom had learned that the hard way the first time they had driven in bad weather. They had sped through a puddle and oddly, the plastic floor mats under their feet had billowed like sails, then a huge wave of cold, muddy water had surged up at them through the floor, scaring them half to death.

Drenched to their socks, they had driven back home very slowly to avoid another swim. Mom had laughed at the whole affair. For reasons Jamie couldn't fathom, she seemed as fond of the old death-trap-on-wheels as you'd be of an old relative: she loved it, even though occasionally it drove her mad.

At the time, he had thought the 'puddle incident' was funny, so he had told his classmates as soon as he had gotten to school. He had regretted it since. For a long time afterward, whenever his mom had dropped him off at school, they had laughed at him and called her a bum behind his back. Jamie had felt furious—his classmates were mean, but he was stupid for telling them. Hadn't he learned it wasn't OK to mention he was poor? Why did he keep forgetting it? Or was he pretending it actually didn't matter?

The muffled sound of splashing water filtered through the plastic floor mats. Jamie put down his feet as Maddie accelerated. He shifted uncomfortably, wondering how far the rust could have eaten the floor around him. He was terrified one day the whole seat would sink in as they were speeding and he'd die in a fury of sparks and grinding metal. He shook his head. Sheesh, we're having some pretty apocalyptic thoughts this morning, Jamie, aren't we?

It always surprised him how certain things could pop into his mind. His own thoughts were an infinite source of wonder to him and trying to figure out why he would ever think that way was equally engaging. It was like following a trail barely marked under the falling snow: the more you went on, the less you could see the path ahead, yet you knew it was there leading you somewhere.

Thelma rattled nastily on a down-shift. Jamie felt his brain come off the hinges. After another few minutes of suffering, they finally arrived at school.

He kissed his mom and opened the door of the car.

"Wait a sec," Maddie said.

He turned and saw her pulling out a ten dollar bill from her pocket.

"Here. Don't say anything to your father."

He nodded. He had no intention of doing so. It was such an excruciating experience to ask him for money that he always preferred to wait for Mom to slip him some dollars every once in a while.

"Bye, Mom."

"Bye, kitten. See you later."

He climbed out of the car and walked into school.

As he entered his classroom, Sara Winters greeted him.

Sara was a tall, brown-haired girl with an intelligent gaze. She was the smartest in the class and they always sat together. He liked talking to her, but unfortunately they had very little in common other than their love of learning, so their exchanges did not go further than school.

He sat down at his desk. He noticed that she already had her math books out and was looking at him with an eager expression. He knew what it meant: she had probably aced her homework, but needed to make sure. "Did you finish the math assignment?" he asked.

"Yeah, I think I did well."

"Do you want to compare?"

"Sure."

Jamie took out his notebook. A familiar giggle made him look up. Holly appeared at the door, hand in hand with Francesca Willson. Puzzled, he stared at the pair of them for a second before he could take in what he was actually seeing: they looked like twins! They had the same hairstyle, same shoes, same skirt, same blouse—even the same socks. Why did they do that? Why would they want to look the same?

He studied their outfits. Francesca looked better. She was very pretty, probably the prettiest girl in the whole school, and that set of clothes suited her best. Holly instead looked strange. She didn't look like herself. It dawned on him that perhaps it was actually just Holly who had dressed up as Francesca. Why would she do that? Girls were so weird...

He kept looking up at Holly as she and Francesca passed by, apparently not noticing him. He watched them as they sat down together on the other side of the classroom. He was still hurt by what had happened the day before and wanted to make peace, so he waited until Holly put down her backpack and finally looked up, then waved his hand at her. Holly startled and tossed up her hand impatiently.

That was a pretty lame hello, he thought. Now she wasn't even going to say hi anymore? Great...

"Quiet!" hissed a velvety, poisonous voice behind him.

The classroom went suddenly silent.

Jamie turned and saw Ms. Ambrose, his teacher, standing at

the door, glaring. She was an elegant brunette in her mid forties with burning eyes and a skinny figure. She was so skinny in fact as to almost look gaunt. He always thought that she looked like something was eating her from the inside. Whatever that was, he hoped never to catch it.

"Good morning, Ms. Ambrose," he said together with the rest of the class. It still felt weird to greet her so formally—especially because she rarely answered back—but she had insisted the whole class did it since she became their teacher in third grade, so it had become almost second nature for them. Jamie wondered once again how different things could have been if he hadn't had Ms. Ambrose for the last three years. His mom had told him once that when she was a girl, she had a different teacher every year of elementary school. That had sounded amazing.

Ms. Ambrose walked to her desk and scanned the classroom for trouble—she immediately spotted Francesca and Holly. She looked them up and down with a smirk, then ordered, "Holly, close the door."

Jamie frowned. Holly sat on the other side of the classroom. Ms. Ambrose usually told him to go because he was closer. Why the change today? He watched Holly blush and spring up nervously, then scuttle to the door, all the way smoothing her dress and hair. She looked very self-conscious. A few stains of sweat started spreading on her back and under her armpits. She noticed and blushed scarlet. Jamie was suddenly hit by a pang of embarrassment for her.

Ms. Ambrose didn't say anything, but watched her with a sarcastic smirk.

Holly slinked back to her desk and sat down sheepishly. She looked like she wanted to disappear through the floor.

Jamie wondered if that was the reason Ms. Ambrose had sent her to the door. Did she want to parade Holly in front of the class and humiliate her? That was so strange. Yet, by the look of things, she had done it on purpose and Holly was definitely mortified. He couldn't really grasp what was going on, but he could sense something mean had just happened. He felt bad for Holly. Even if she didn't say hello to him anymore, she didn't deserve such treatment. She had just dressed up like her best friend. Maybe it was strange—I mean, it was strange—but why make her feel so bad about it?

The creaking of Ms. Ambrose's leather bag made him turn. He saw her pull out a stack of paper and place it on her desk. The air in the classroom suddenly went sour. Those were the history essays. Jamie prayed he got a decent grade. History was his favorite subject and one in which he could hold his own against Sara. They were the best of the class, but she usually got the better grades.

Ms. Ambrose beckoned him.

Jamie stood up and walked to the desk.

"Hand them out to the class," she said, passing him the stack of paper.

Jamie picked up the essays, thankful to have something to do instead of being stuck at his desk, sweating his way through the minutes it took to get his own paper. He tried not to peek at his classmates' grades, but guessed many of them by the reactions on their faces.

When he arrived at Holly and Francesca's desks, he couldn't resist anymore. He picked up the papers with deliberate slowness, giving himself the time to recognize the red ink scribble. Holly had gotten a B, Francesca only a C. Jamie smiled—they may look the same, but Holly was smarter. He didn't know why, but it gave him pleasure to know that. Hope maybe? For what? That Holly would reconsider and say hello to him again? Yes, definitely! And also hope that she'd figure out that twin affair. She didn't need to look like somebody else. She was pretty and smart on her own. He watched her smiling at the red B on her paper.

Francesca leaned in, frowning. "How come you got a B?

Holly glanced up, alarmed.

Jamie feigned he didn't hear. He moved up one desk, but kept his eyes on them.

Francesca pinched Holly's arm viciously. "You saved the good stuff for yourself, didn't you?"

Holly flinched. "No. I didn't. I don't know why—"

Francesca scoffed and turned away.

Oh yes, thought Jamie, she knew very well why Francesca had gotten a worse grade. She knew she was smarter, that's why, but she couldn't say it, otherwise Francesca would write her off.

He sat down at his desk and glanced back at them. Holly looked mortified again; she leaned in apologetically and whispered something in Francesca's ear, who shrugged her off. Seriously, why did Holly hang out with her and instead didn't even say hi to him anymore?

He finally looked down at his own essay. A red B+ blotted the paper. Yes! A wave of relief ran through him. He looked up at Sara to see whether this time he had won their little unspoken competition. It looked like it. She was frowning cross-armed at her own paper, huffing grumpily, unable to contain her disappointment. As soon as she realized he was staring at her, she shot him a look.

"B. I only got a B! I spent a whole week working on this," she said, stabbing the paper accusatorily with her index finger.

"It's just bad luck."

"Yeah, but you got a B-plus!"

"Well... sure, but it's still not one of your As."

Sara waved his comment aside and turned around.

Jamie was taken aback. What was wrong with her? Did she

mean he wasn't smart enough to get a better grade than her for once?

Sara turned around. She raised her eyes nervously up into his. "Sorry..."

He nodded. He didn't know what to say, but his anger faded away. Sara was nice. Thank goodness. It was almost funny how upset she was—she still got a good grade. She was so tough on herself—too tough. She liked only As and he knew she would torment herself until the next test. He wished he cared as much about grades as she did. In the end, he didn't. He couldn't study for a grade. Either he liked what he was studying or he'd invariably do a lousy job. He had tried many times, but it was like swimming against the flow. It never worked and he hated it. He felt spoiled behaving like that, childish, so he forced himself when he couldn't stand the topic or the subject. It was all he could do really.

Ms. Ambrose leaned back in her chair and crossed her arms. "Let's see if you have done your homework," she said with a hint of menace in her voice.

The class, apart from Jamie and Sara, cowered back.

He sat up, eager to hear the question. This was his favorite part. Whenever there was some kind of discussion, he enjoyed himself. Learning things by heart was boring and sitting at a desk all morning instead of playing outside was even more boring. What he liked was learning to think and discussions were one of the best ways to do that, so he welcomed any sort of engagement. It was mostly him who raised his hand in class, so there wasn't much competition or excitement in answering, but that didn't bother him. Even Sara only raised her hand sparingly. Perhaps it was because she was shier than him.

"What battle had the highest number of casualties in the Civil War?" asked Ms. Ambrose. "And here's a hint: it was here in Pennsylvania."

Jamie knew that one easily. It wasn't the kind of question he would have liked, since it only required him to remember something, but at least there was something to talk about. He raised his hand.

The rest of the morning went by pretty smoothly. He answered some more questions in history class, then raised his hand a few more times in geography class. By the time recess came, he felt like he had managed not to get bored to death.

The bell rang.

Jamie carefully opened his lunch box and scooped out his pie. Despite Thelma's treacherous attempt to destroy it, it was still in one piece. He smiled: this time he would enjoy the pie and keep it down too. He left the classroom and headed down the hallway.

As he arrived at the door, he spotted the third-grader he had helped the day before waving his hand, headed toward him.

He nodded and waited for him. He felt a knot in his stomach tighten.

"Hi!" the boy said stretching out his hand

Jamie took it and relaxed a bit. "Hi!"

"I'm Alan."

"Jamie. Nice to meet you."

Alan lowered his eyes. "I... I just wanted to say I'm sorry I was rude yesterday. I know you were just trying to help."

"No problem. I'm glad you got away from those three."

Alan looked up. "I think I could have gotten my notebook back by myself, but I still wanted to thank you for helping me out."

Jamie grinned—he didn't stand a chance, but he liked his courage. "Next time, you'll help me out. Deal?"

Alan grinned "Deal. I'll see you around then, Jamie."

"See you."

Alan turned around and ran up the stairs.

See, he thought, Holly was wrong. Alan didn't think he was rude. He appreciated his help.

"Jamie!" called a voice behind him.

He turned around and saw Francesca walking up to him. Everybody wants to talk to me today, he joked with himself. Francesca, though, usually ignored him. Maybe she had come to ask him if he wanted to eat lunch with her and Holly. That would be great. He smiled. "Hi!"

Francesca didn't smile back.

He noticed, but his smile remained glued on his face like an ictus. A few feet behind her, he spotted Holly waiting impatiently. He nodded toward her. She looked away.

"You need to stop," Francesca broke out bluntly.

Jamie's smile dissolved. "Stop what?"

"Raising your hand. You're making us all look bad."

"I wasn't trying to make anybody look bad."

"I don't care. You're making us look stupid and you must stop."

Was Francesca talking about her and Holly? he wondered. He couldn't believe Holly thought that. If Francesca didn't want to look stupid, then maybe she should raise her hand instead of being lazy! And why now? He had been raising his hand since first grade and nobody had ever complained before. "You can't—"

"Oh yes, I can. I am the class rep. We voted. We're tired of you making us look bad."

Jamie winced. They voted? She meant the whole class had voted? Everybody? They all thought that?

Francesca gestured Holly to follow her and they walked away without saying good-bye.

Jamie stood nailed to the spot, his head swimming and swaying in a pool of boiling anger. How dare they telling him what he could and could not do? Why did he have to listen to them? They didn't have the right to tell him what to do. We voted, Francesca's voice echoed in his mind. They voted... So, if he didn't listen to them, what would they do? He didn't want to listen to them, but he didn't want to be singled out either. Answering questions was the only thing that made school bearable. Why were they doing that to him? Why didn't they tell him before? Why had nobody ever talked to him about it? They had just voted behind his back!

Jamie suddenly realized he was squashing Mom's apple pie in his fist. He willed himself to relax his hand. He didn't want to waste another piece of pie—it was probably the only slice of sympathy he would get today.

5

LUNCH WITH DAD

Maddie waved at Jamie from across the street. He disentangled himself from the throng of other kids pouring out of the school gate and crossed toward her.

"Hi, Mom."

"Hi, dear," she answered, jumping in the car.

She seemed in a hurry, he thought. Better that way. It would be easier to hide how he felt. He was still too angry to talk about what had happened.

Old Thelma lurched forward, rattling like a crate of scrap metal. Jamie felt the familiar vibration fill his ears and insides, making him queasy. He put a hand on his belly and winced as a rancid bubble of apple and acids popped in his mouth—disgusting. He swallowed back quickly, trying to forget what a torture it was to have the once-wonderful flavor of the pie twisted and regurgitated into something so vile.

"Everything all right at school?" Maddie asked.

"Yeah," he said laconically. Then he caught himself and felt the sudden need to add something. He didn't want her to press on. He didn't want to talk about what Francesca had told him. "I got B-plus in history."

Maddie beamed at him. "That's great! And you love history. You see, you're always afraid of orals, but then you do well."

"It was the essay, not the oral."

"Oh... You had a test?"

"Yeah, it was last week."

Maddie's expression sagged. "Sorry, I forgot."

Jamie shrugged.

"What was it about again?"

"It was about patronage," he said without looking at her—Francesca's words were still ringing in his ears. "How patrons helped artists in the Renaissance. And the difference with sponsors today."

"Nice. I wish there were still patrons for artists today. "It was a good deal. Or at least it seemed so."

Jamie nodded and he remembered that Mom had been a dancer once, but she had injured her ankle and had to quit. He wondered whether his own life would also turn against him. We voted, Francesca's words echoed in his mind. He stared out of the side window, watching the houses and fields streak past, hoping some of his bad mood would get caught between the bricks and the weeds.

Finally, they arrived home. Jamie got out of the car and opened the iron gate.

Maddie drove all the way up to the kitchen door. She turned off the engine and shot out of the car.

Jamie saw her rush inside. He frowned. His father must have come back from a trip to his horse feed clients and asked for lunch even if it was late. And Mom had probably left the stove on to have the food ready when they got back.

As soon as he put a foot in the kitchen, he heard his father yell, "Is it ready!?" from the bedroom on the other side of the house, where the TV was blaring, while Mom was scraping some potatoes off a burnt pan. It was at moments like this that Jamie thought his parents were actually insane. His mom had left the stove on for something like half an hour while she drove out to get him—which was obviously dangerous. And his father had sat in the bedroom all this time, preferring not to make the effort (and what effort exactly were we talking about here?) to walk to the kitchen and check that the whole house wouldn't burn down. That was plain crazy.

"Yes, it's ready! Come here!" Maddie yelled back.

Jamie walked in. "Can I help you?"

"No, it's OK. Sit down."

He'd rather go upstairs and eat his sandwich alone, but Mom always insisted they eat together whenever they could, since they were all on different schedules. He sat at the table.

Maddie passed him a ham sandwich.

Again, he thought with resignation.

His father, Jan Blackshear, finally walked into the kitchen. He was a blue-eyed, straight-haired, well-built man. He stood in the door frame and looked around disgusted. "You made a mess again."

"I'll clean," Maddie answered curtly. "Sit down or it'll get cold."

Why his dad was so obsessed with cleaning, Jamie couldn't figure out, especially because he wouldn't clean anything unless it was to show him and his mom that they were very dirty. Why did he not clean up while Mom was out if he was so disgusted by it? But, as usual, he hadn't lifted a finger.

"Hi, chicken," he said, slapping him on the back of the head.

Jamie felt a wave of rage at the gesture and had to fight it down. "Hi, Dad," he said stiffly.

Jan sat down.

Maddie handed him a plate of spaghetti drowned in tomato sauce.

"Pasta? Again?"

"I didn't have time to do anything else."

He scoffed and poured himself a glass of beer. He swallowed it whole and burped.

"Jan!" Maddie shouted.

He winked at Jamie with a defiant grin and poured himself another glass of beer.

Jamie kept a neutral face. When he was little, he thought his father was funny. Now he mostly found him annoying, if not outright rude. He knew Mom didn't like his father burping, that she thought it was a bad example for him. Apparently his dad liked to give him the bad example.

"Where's the cheese?" he asked, looking around as if he was at a restaurant with really bad service.

Jamie watched his mom stand up. Was it really necessary? Why did he always have to behave like he was the king of France? The bowl with the grated cheese was two feet away on the kitchen counter, well in sight. Why couldn't he stand up and get it like anybody else? He hated the way he always ordered them around.

"Here!" Maddie passed Jan the cheese and sat down again.

"It's overcooked," he said after tasting the spaghetti.

Maddie didn't answer.

They ate in silence.

Jamie could feel his father's eyes on him.

"Did you get any good grades today?"

Jamie didn't look up from his plate. What does he care? "I got a B-plus."

"Not an A, but not too shabby."

Jamie shrugged—of course that wasn't good enough for him. "I don't care about grades that much anyway."

"Oh yeah, you're too good for that, uh!?"

Jamie startled and glanced up. His father was glaring down at him. He panicked. Why on Earth did he say that? He shouldn't have said that! He looked away and mumbled, "No..."

"Grades aren't that important, right?" cut in Maddie. "It's more important that he learns."

Jan scoffed. "How is he going to get a scholarship then, eh? I'm not going to let him leech off of us forever."

"He got a good grade, Jan." Maddie sighed. "Stop worrying."

"Yeah, right..."

"So, how's the deal with Franklin going anyway? Is he buying Stinger or we can put him back on rotation in the school?"

Thanks Mom, Jamie thought.

"It's all right," Jan replied while he poured himself another glass of beer. "I'll head up to him tomorrow and see to it. He's just trying to be smart with me."

That was already three glasses of beer in less than ten minutes, Jamie counted. That was too much, wasn't it? He glanced up and saw that his father's eyes looked hazy—yes, it was. He glanced back down at his sandwich—he couldn't imagine anything more unappealing at the moment. All the hunger in his stomach had been strangled away by tension, leaving in its place a tight knot. Man, he really needed Acorn.

Maddie picked up Jan's empty plate. "Do you want some chicken?"

"As long as it's edible."

She surveyed the half burnt potatoes and selected the few intact ones, then she grabbed two dry looking chicken thighs from the stove. She stuffed everything on a plate and brought it back on the table.

Jan glared at the food in front of him.

Jamie took a bite of his sandwich and shoveled it down his throat. He swallowed it almost without chewing.

"Eat slowly," Maddie said.

He nodded, but had no intention of listening to her. He took another bite and swallowed it as quickly as possible. He couldn't leave any food on the plate—that was another thing that annoyed his father. But then, what didn't?

The phone rang.

Maddie ran into the living room and picked up. "Jamie, it's for you!" she called.

He looked up, puzzled. For him? Strange. They probably just got the wrong number, or it was a prank from some of his classmates. He braced himself for that. In any case, it was better than sitting at the table with his father. He went into the living room and picked up the phone.

"Hello?"

"Hi Jamie. It's Dan."

Dan? Dan Muldbridge? Maybe he just needed to ask him about homework or something. "Hey, what's up?"

"Nothing. Wanna come over watch some TV?"

"TV? No way!" Whoa, that came out much harsher than he had meant it to. It was true though: he felt cooped up and needed some fresh air. He needed to move and forget and have fun—he couldn't really stand the idea of sitting in front of a TV. He felt his whole body aching just thinking about it.

Dan, on the other end of the line, fell silent.

Jamie felt torn. He really wanted to go out with Acorn, but it wasn't every day that somebody offered to hang out with him. The thing was that he and Dan had almost nothing in common and he found it strange that he called him to hang out. "Do you want to go to the river instead?" he said on a whim. Then he remembered Dan didn't like physical activities. He was clumsy and very self-conscious. He had never seen him enjoy any outdoor games at school.

"I don't know..."

"It'll be fun, I promise."

"Hmm…"

For a second, Jamie thought of giving in, but he couldn't bring himself to it. "Just come to the river. If you don't like it, we'll go back to your place, OK?" He could always get out of that, he thought, if he really needed. Just blame Acorn or something.

"Oh… OK," Dan said.

"Cool. See you in a bit."

"See ya."

6

RIVER

Jamie whizzed around the bend at full speed. The wheels of his bike whooshed on the dirt road, sending pebbles shooting into the woods. He cleared a hump, flying a few inches from the ground, then locked the brakes and skidded to a halt. He turned around.

After a few seconds, Dan appeared, standing on the pedals of his bicycle, visibly worn out. Probably because he couldn't take it anymore, he sat back down and rode over a big slate of rock. His bike reared up, then jerked down on the other side of the obstacle, whiplashing his back. Dan grimaced and pulled himself up again.

A pang of guilt mixed with impatience gripped Jamie. He should have never brought Dan to the river—he was clearly uncomfortable in the outdoors. He watched him negotiate another rock and was surprised once again by how vaguely girly he looked. Dan had straight brown hair that fell around his round face. He was chubby—not overweight, but definitely plump—with pale skin that never seemed to tan. His blue eyes were huge, as big and round as those of the girls in their class, and they seemed constantly terrified of whatever they were looking at.

There was something delicate, fragile about him that Jamie couldn't explain. He didn't mind that. Actually, he kind of liked it, even if it meant Dan wasn't cut out for the outdoors, because it seemed like a unique quality.

Dan resembled one of those oversensitive horses that his father sometimes took home: animals way too touchy that often ended up being too difficult to handle and had to be sold out of the riding school. Dan wasn't exactly like that—he was nice, actually too nice to be fair—but he seemed as thin-skinned as those horses. So, perhaps that was what they both had in common after all: they were both sensitive people.

Jamie knew he was. It was the reason why he could communicate with animals and feel them. Nevertheless, he was aware that he and Dan were not at all alike. He couldn't picture Dan being able to feel an animal. Maybe a person, but certainly not an animal. His sensibility looked like something else altogether. And the big problem was that it totally overwhelmed him. It was as if this sensibility defined him, leaving no space for anything else.

In fact, he recollected that he had never seen Dan get angry or show any type of toughness at school. That was why he attracted so much bullying from the other boys. He had this delicate quality about him and no defenses whatsoever. He was living bait for bullies.

Dan groaned impatiently and dismounted his bike.

Jamie frowned. "What are you doing?"

"I'll just walk."

"It's only another five minutes to the river. Come on!"

Dan tucked in his chin and kept pushing his bike stubbornly, unwilling to get back on.

Jamie slapped a hand on his thigh. Oh, come on, he thought,

you're not my grandma! Give me a break! It wasn't that difficult to ride on the path. His sympathy toward Dan suddenly plummeted. He didn't like whiners and Dan was definitely acting like one.

He spun around and sprinted forward. What a waste of time! The river was literally five minutes away. Would it cost Dan so much to keep on going? He wasn't going to die! Sure, but he never wanted to come in the first place, so...

Jamie pulled the brakes and stopped. Right... Dan had come only to do him a favor and he was being a jerk. Calm down, he ordered himself. It had been a bad idea. He should have gone out with Acorn or by himself—probably better by himself, at least at first, to take the edge off.

He wanted to be nice, but he felt he couldn't contain his frenzy. He needed to let it all out, run, strain himself, feel his heart and lungs burn, before he could feel better. How was he going to do that with Dan around? He looked over his shoulder and saw him get back on his bike, then, slowly and carefully, start pedaling again on the very edge of the dirt road where there was still some sand and soft ground, instead of the exposed rocks.

Jamie's hopes for their hike lifted again. He waited for Dan to catch up with him, then started riding slowly alongside.

A rumbling breeze welcomed them as they finally arrived at the embankments. Jamie felt the air come forward in waves, brushing his face, curling and swirling like the mirror image of the foaming river nearby. The wind carried up to him a tangy odor of running water, fish and reeds that he loved.

Dan dropped his bike.

Jamie dismounted and ran to the edge of the raised embankment. He breathed in a lungful of crispy, swirling air and looked down. On his left, the river dam, a gray mass of cement, ran from one shore to the other like the huge collar of a fierce beast. The black inflatable tube that crowned it had been deflated today, letting the water glide over its edge and down the cement slide on the other side. Massive pillars of reinforced concrete waited at the bottom, ready to break the current. It was there that the full power of the river was in display: enormous foaming waves reared up against the pillars, roaring and struggling with the sound of a charging army. Walls of water clashed against each other, then plunged into whirlpools and exploded out again. Like water dragons, the waves thrashed around until they broke the chains laid upon them by humans, then swam away and disappeared under the liquid veil of the river. They were always there, though, dangerous and unpredictable, poised to swallow you if you dared to challenge them.

Jamie loved the river exactly for that reason—the same reason why he loved mountains and wild animals—because it was as formidable as it was beautiful and it demanded respect, humility and courage if you wanted to be in its company.

He turned to Dan. "Isn't it gorgeous?"

He glanced at him, then turned back at the dam. He seemed to struggle to take it all in. "Looks scary."

"Yeah, I know," Jamie grinned. He sprinted forward and hopped down the massive steps of the embankment.

Dan followed more carefully, supporting himself against the metal mesh that held in the river rocks and pebbles. These nets resembled oversize steps and were embedded in the flanks of the river in order to avoid landslides. Dan lowered himself, taking care not to trip and get cut.

Near the riverbed, the roar of the dam was deafening. Jamie stood at the edge of the water, facing the chaos of clashing waves forty yards away. He opened his arms and closed his eyes. A fine mist whipped his skin like wet sand shot from a cannon while the whirling winds tugged him around.

Dan stood next to him, holding his sweater tight around his neck. "It's cold," he shouted.

"I know," Jamie yelled back, throwing back his arms. "Feel it. It's awesome!"

Dan hesitated, shivering, then he stretched out his arms too. He started laughing.

Jamie smiled. "How's that!?"

"It's crazy!"

"I know. It's like a roller coaster!"

He closed his eyes and relished the thundering, misty gale. He felt the low rumble of the water carrying not only through the air, but also through the ground where he was standing. Such power, he thought. Together, the air, sound and smell of the place were like a shot of excitement. He could feel his body smile as if it had just received a Christmas present. He opened his eyes.

Dan beckoned him, shivering. "I'm off, too cold!"

"OK."

They walked downstream, away from the deafening thunder of the dam. Spring had just started, so the river was not in full flood yet, leaving two large strips of its banks available as walkways. Boulders, rocks and pebbles of all sizes stretched ahead for some three miles before disappearing into the woods where the river took a turn to the left.

As the chaos behind him faded away, so did Jamie's excitement. He peeled his eyes off of the rocky bank and looked up, searching for a new rush. Next to him, the river flowed with a low growl. Some fifty yards away, a strip of trees and rocks shone blazing white and green, emerging from the running waters like a mystic island. On the opposite shore, dark shadows hung between the branches of thick woods.

Jamie sighed and turned away from the scenery. A great view really, but it wasn't enough. He absolutely needed to do something, to sweat the bad day out or he'd explode. He searched the place for an idea. There wasn't much around that he could use to play with Dan, just rocks, rocks, rocks. He wasn't going to stone Dan, so... Well, they could skip. It was a little bit of a stretch for Dan, but maybe...

"Have you ever done pebble skipping?" he asked, turning around.

"You mean throwing rocks?"

"No, I mean skip on the rocks and pebbles. Run and hop, you know. It's fun!" He gestured invitingly toward the rocks on the trail.

Dan frowned.

"It's amazing, really," he went on. "Always look forward, so you see what's coming and you can think where you'll put your foot next. You start slow, then you speed up and try to keep a straight line in the air as if you were hanging from a rope and just used the rocks to push yourself forward. At a certain point, you reach cruising speed and it's awesome—it's like flying!" He made a hovering gesture with his hand. "You're just brushing the rocks and gliding airborne—"

"Air what?"

Jamie lost his train of thought. "Airborne. I think it means flying. Like born in the air, you know."

"Why didn't you just say flying?"

Jamie shrugged.

Dan shrugged back and looked away.

Jamie faltered. Their conversation had derailed somewhere really unexpected. He felt uncomfortable. OK, he thought, no more funny words. He mustered what he hoped was an exciting smile and patted Dan on the shoulder. "So, you wanna try?"

He frowned. "What if you fall?"

"Well, the trick is not to fall."

Dan shook his head.

"Look, if you fall, you let yourself fall and throw your hands out. Otherwise, you'll just hurt yourself. Use your hands and arms to slow down, then roll if you can. If you can't, turn on your side and use your shoulder as a cushion. It's not that hard really."

As soon as he finished speaking, he caught his own lie. Not that hard? Well, that wasn't true actually. He was used to falling from horses, trees, fences, bikes and a thousand other things. He had made it into an art, but Dan probably hadn't even fallen from a chair before. Well, maybe from a chair, but he was sure that if that had happened, Dan had probably hurt himself.

"I'll just watch you," he replied, sitting on a boulder.

Jamie felt his temper rise. He didn't want to have to sit with him. "Come on, you can do it!"

Dan shook his head.

A new wave of frenzy gripped Jamie. He needed to go now. "Fine. You're just missing out."

Dan looked away.

Jamie flushed. Couldn't he just shut up? He whirled around and jumped blindly. He zeroed in on not falling on his face and blocked out everything else. He focused his eyes a few feet in front of him, then started hopping from one rock to the next. Quickly, he reached cruising speed. Brushing with his long legs against the rocks, he resembled a weird marsh treader propelling itself forward on an invisible surface.

Gliding airborne, he watched the rocks and pebbles rush toward him, deciding where to put his foot next in a fraction of a second. It felt like a dance to him, an extremely fast tip-tap. It was an all-consuming task you could not take your eyes off of even to blink. He felt all of his body and his mind coil and uncoil at each step, burning together. It was exactly what he needed. And he wanted more. He pushed himself, then pushed himself again and again, but his reflexes would not give in. Today he was as quick as lightning.

At last, he stopped and looked back: Dan was a little dot in the distance. Wow, he must have run at full speed for almost a mile! That was probably his new record. He grinned and shifted his attention to his body. His heart was thundering in his chest and his lungs hurt. Everything inside him was buzzing with pleasure and pain. A rush of oxygen ran through him like a sugar high. He felt alive, gloriously alive. Thank goodness Dan didn't want to follow him—he was just acting crazy. At that rate, he would have gotten him out of his depths and into disaster.

He turned back to the river. The water looked calm and beautiful like an uninterrupted slate of glass. Yet, it was not still at all. Its current could jam you against a rock and hold you there, squeezing all the air out of you until it turned you into a heap of limp flesh, dead as stone.

Nature was simply incredible, Jamie thought. What surrounded him on every corner was pure, majestic, alive beauty. And he was part of it. He was. That was what thrilled him most, what made him feel alive. Heaven, just like Mom said, was not up in the clouds where you could never die, it was here among the roaring water and the rocks where you could die but you felt alive.

He smiled and took a big breath, slowing down his pulse. A rock emerging from the water a few feet away from him caught his attention. The slab of chipped stone was close enough that you could maybe reach it with a long jump, but far enough that you could miss it and plunge into the river.

He considered whether it was worth the risk. The stream embraced the rock tightly like a toddler squeezing his favorite toy—a sleeper hold. With the dam open, the current was strong. If he plunged into the river in the wrong spot, it could be lethal. The water was also cold and, given its force, it would take him a good mile or two to get back on dry land if he didn't drown first. The odds were against him. He turned back and waved his hand at Dan.

After a second's hesitation, Dan waved back.

Jamie took a big breath and retraced his steps at a more leisurely pace.

As he reached Dan, he noticed with relief that he didn't seem annoyed and was just studying him curiously as if watching a strange animal with foreign habits.

"Are you thirsty?" Dan asked.

"Yeah, sure. Wanna go to the store next to the dam?"

"They have sodas, right?"

"I think so. I mean, they have an angling pond and everything. I guess they have drinks and chips, and other stuff."

Dan seemed to cheer up at the idea of junk food. Jamie didn't mind either. Some sugar would make the afternoon even sweeter. His hand felt about in his jeans pocket, getting hold of the ten dollar bill his mom had given him.

The store was a very bare-bones establishment with unpainted cement walls, two small windows and a small counter. And it was cold, Jamie noticed as they entered. Probably because of the thick concrete it was made of. He blinked, trying to adjust his eyes to the dim light. He turned to Dan, who seemed to have the same reaction. They both looked around and took in the place.

Jamie caught sight of the chips stand and made a beeline for it. Chips or drink, he wondered. Well, if he got the chips, he had to drink something, otherwise he would die of thirst. He scanned the rack and spotted his favorite flavor in the whole universe: Cheddar and Sour Cream Ruffles. He felt his stomach gape open. This day was definitely making a comeback! He needed those chips; it was a matter of life and death. Or was it? All of a sudden, his enthusiasm flickered—wasn't he actually just wasting his money? Yes, he was. He knew that, but he didn't want to think about it. He just wanted to have a good time and pretend he could waste some dollars if he felt like it. He snapped the Ruffles off the rack and marched to the counter. No going back now.

Dan peeled himself off of the ice cream sign on the wall and joined him.

Jamie was surprised to find the owner of the bar, a tall, scraggy man, staring back morosely at them. His untidy black hair lay shapeless around a face lined with deep wrinkles—he looked like a plowed field. His mouth was bent down at the corners in a grimace of displeasure, or maybe it was sadness. Jamie thought that the man looked as mean as an iron poker. His sparse black beard made him queasy. He couldn't see the man's hands, but he was convinced his fingernails were dirty.

"Hello!" Dan said politely.

The man's face unfroze. The corners of his mouth twisted upward in a smile. His eyes lit up with intelligence. "What can I get you, boys?" he said in a warm, pleasant drawl.

The change startled Jamie.

"A Coke, please," Dan said.

The store owner nodded and bent down behind the counter.

"Another one too, please," Jamie added, recovering from his surprise.

The man straightened up and pushed two tin cans toward them on the counter. "There you go," he said with a grin. "Nice and fresh—just picked." He patted the metal of the Coke cans and chuckled at his own light joke.

His hands were not dirty at all, Jamie noticed. They were instead well taken care of. A smooth golden band shone on his ring finger. Somebody must love him, Jamie thought. He always found it strange when he saw wedding rings on the fingers of adults. He wondered how that felt, to have someone think that you're so special.

"Anything else, gentlemen?"

Dan raised his hand. "A cone for me."

Jamie looked up and patted his chips fondly. "I've got these babies!"

The man chuckled. "Excellent choice." He turned back toward Dan and said, "Cone incoming," then walked off.

Jamie and Dan glanced at each other with raised highbrows. The dude was weird, there was no question about it. Nevertheless, Jamie was starting to like him. The man was obviously enjoying their little chat very much. A little too much actually. Perhaps he was lonely and that was why he looked so down in the dumps. Jamie felt a little sad they were going to leave him alone again. He also felt guilty he judged him so harshly at first. Maybe the man just had a bad day like him or he was worried about something.

They watched him step up to an old industrial freezer and rummage inside for the cone.

Suddenly, Dan stretched forward like a pointer dog at the smell of game.

Jamie saw him pat his jeans, as if to make sure he hadn't dropped his wallet. Then he threw a fleeting glance back at him and craned over the counter.

The store owner had just extracted an icy cone from the freezer and was bringing it up to the counter.

"Can I have that big bottle of Coke too?" Dan asked, pointing to the ground.

The man stopped in his tracks and scooped up a two liter Coke bottle from a small rack. "This? It's warm though."

"It's all right."

"You must be thirsty, boy. Sure you don't want a couple of cold ones? Tell you what, I'll cut you a deal. Same price."

Dan flushed. "I like the big bottle."

"Fair enough." The man handed him the bottle with a puzzled look.

Jamie couldn't blame him. He was puzzled too. Was Dan going to drink the whole bottle by himself? Fine that he liked sodas, but that was a bit too much for one person. He'd get sick. Plus, the bottle was warm. Was he going to cool it off in the river? But Dan would never think of that. And he already had another bottle. It just didn't add up.

The store owner pulled two plastic straws from a dispenser and slid them toward them. "On the house. It's no fun to drink without a straw, right?"

Jamie actually didn't care for straws, but he loved the gesture.

"Thank you," he and Dan said in unison, handing him their money.

When it was time to leave, Jamie hesitated. He wanted to thank the man for his kindness, but he felt too uncomfortable. "Well, good-bye," he mumbled awkwardly.

"Bye," Dan parroted.

The man waved at them.

"Have a good day," Jamie threw in while leaving.

The man smiled sadly. "You too. Have fun in the sun."

Jamie heard real longing in his voice, as if he would have given an arm and a leg to go out in the sun too. Jamie nodded and was off.

As they walked outside, Dan glanced up with a conspiratorial look and whispered, "Do you wanna see something cool?"

It was Jamie's turn to frown this time. Dan's shift of mood made him suspicious. Better play along, he decided. It can't be anything dangerous. It's Dan, after all. "Sure..."

Dan led him to a clearing in the woods nearby that was often used as a parking space. He checked there was nobody around, then sneaked farther into a nook.

This was getting interesting, Jamie thought.

The place was sheltered and cozy. All the trees around them muffled the sounds outside, lending an air of secrecy to this corner of the woods.

"I just need to set it up," Dan said, turning around.

Jamie nodded and followed him.

Dan stopped him. "No, stay here. I'll get it ready, then we can watch."

"Oh, OK..."

Jamie waited as Dan unscrewed the Coke bottle with some effort. He took off the plastic cap and put it in his pocket. He proceeded to smoothen a patch of ground with his foot, then he set the open bottle down. He drew a package of Menthos out of the back pocket of his jeans and turned. "Are you ready?"

Ready for what? Jamie thought. "I guess so..."

"All right." Dan wetted his lips. He picked up five Menthos out of the wrapper and held them in a vertical column between his fingers. He crouched down in front of the Coke bottle and brought his hand flush with the open top.

Jamie kneeled down, watching rapt.

Dan glanced quickly in Jamie's direction as if to calculate the distance between them, then he let the five drops of Menthos plunge all at once into the bottle and sprinted away.

Jamie jumped up and craned his neck. In a matter of seconds, a thick foam formed inside the bottle and the Coke erupted in a two-foot soda geyser.

"Whoa!" he shouted, astonished.

Dan pumped his fist in the air and let out a satisfied, "Yessss!"

The erupting bottle shook violently on the uneven terrain and toppled over. Propelled by the pressure of the foaming soda, it skidded on the ground, shooting into the woods like a projectile.

Dan and Jamie followed its trajectory, screaming and laughing at the same time.

The bottle hit a tree, ricocheted, flung itself against another tree, lost its momentum, then whirled around on the ground like a mad snake, finally fizzing to a silent death.

Jamie and Dan stood in awe for a second, then ran up to the bottle, jumping and screaming.

"Did you see that?" Jamie shouted, elbowing Dan.

"Yeah. I told you it was cool!"

"No, it was awesome! That was amazing! Whooosh!" He made the gesture of the bottle flying through the air. "How did you do it?"

"I don't know. You just drop in the Menthos and it does that."

"Wow," Jamie exclaimed as if the explanation said it all. "How did you figure it out?"

"One time, I was just eating one," Dan gesticulated with the Menthos wrapper in his hand, "and I drank Coke. I thought my mouth was about to explode. So, I dropped some in a bottle to see if I was crazy or something."

"Super cool!"

Dan grinned and held up the Menthos. "Want one?"

"Totally."

They took one each and savored them as if that could give them more insight in how this all worked.

The Menthos hurt Jamie's palate with its chemical freshness. It tasted awesome, so of course it was going to make awesome things, he thought. He picked up the bottle and they headed out of the patch of wood.

As Dan was putting the wrapper in his jeans' pocket, a Menthos slipped out and fell on the ground. He grumbled, but didn't pick it up.

"Do you mind if I take it?" Jamie asked.

Dan raised his brows. "You gonna eat it? I can give you another one."

Jamie blushed. He didn't like that Dan thought he was so poor he needed to pick up food from the ground. "It's not for me," he said stiffly. He blew on the Menthos to remove the dirt. "It's for Acorn. A little present."

Dan frowned. "Isn't it bad for animals to eat candy?"

Jamie shrugged. "I don't know. He likes it."

"You don't know? You've got all those animals…"

Jamie shrugged again. "He's never been sick, so I think it's fine."

Dan looked unconvinced.

Jamie sighed. Why did people always assume he knew everything about animals? He knew a lot for sure, but he wasn't a vet. "I mean. I heard our vet say once not to give chocolate to dogs because it's poison for them. But everybody gives Menthos to their horses at the school. It's like sugar cubes, I guess. The horses love it."

Dan frowned. "I thought it gave them seizures."

"Seizures?" Jamie laughed.

Dan glared at him. "That's what happened with my dog. She died."

Jamie stopped laughing at once. "Oh, I'm sorry." He never knew Dan had a dog. "Horses are fine with candy…"

Dan turned around.

They walked in silence for a while.

Jamie felt bad about having laughed at Dan. He didn't want to ruin the good time they were having. "Have you tried with other stuff?" he asked tentatively, gesturing toward the Coke bottle.

Dan's expression lit up again. "Oh, yeah!" he grinned knowingly.

The sun was setting when Jamie finally got home. The big

lights in the school were already on. As he passed by the hedge, he saw his father fixing a pole in a four fences jumping exercise, while a group of young riders warmed up around him.

Jamie was dying to tell Acorn about his trip to the river, so he hurried past the iron gate. But first, he needed to let his mom know he was back. He leaned his bike against the wall of the house and headed toward the kitchen. As he got closer, a mouth-watering fragrance wafted up to him—there was something good in the oven.

He popped his head inside. "I'm back!"

Mom wasn't there, but the lights and the oven were on. Jamie inhaled deeply. The smell of baked chicken, potatoes, mushroom and rosemary flooded his palate. Mom had made chicken pot pie! There was no better way to end the day than with one of his favorite dishes. His stomach let out a low grumble of anticipation. Mom wasn't in sight, but she was probably upstairs. Jamie turned and shouted, "I'm back!"

"OK!" called Maddie from the upper floor, "dinner's almost ready!"

"I'll just go say hello to Acorn then!"

He didn't know why, but he always had fun yelling back and forth across the house with his mom.

"Did you have fun?" Maddie said, her voice much closer.

Jamie stepped back and looked up at the balcony.

She was smiling at him, leaning over the railing.

He smiled back. "Yes."

"Good." Maddie nodded cheerfully. "I think Acorn is still in the paddock."

"OK. I'll check."

"I'll give you a holler when it's ready. Keep your ears open."

Jamie grinned and raised his thumb—it seemed Mom liked their little shouting game too. He turned and headed toward the paddock.

All in all, this day had really made a comeback. He was surprised at how well things had gone with Dan. Despite the fact that they were so different, they had managed to spend some great time together. If things kept on going like this, maybe they could see each other more often. Maybe they could even become best friends.

He had no idea Dan was so smart. Figuring out the Coke geyser thing wasn't something everybody could do. And the other experiments he had told him about were really cool. He had never imagined Dan was so curious and ingenious. Plus, he had had a dog. Perhaps they had many more things in common than he had first thought. He wondered whether Francesca was also smarter than he looked and not as mean and arrogant and...

He snorted, curbing his rising temper. Calm down, he told himself. Just the thought of her made him see red. Why on Earth did Holly hang out with her? he thought for the thousandth time.

He shook his head. Stop thinking about all the bad stuff, he ordered himself. A nice chicken pot pie is waiting for you in the oven and Acorn is only a few feet away, and it is a wonderful night, and there will be more days like this to come!

With a sigh of relief, he craned his neck over the hedge. Acorn wasn't in sight. He must be in his box, then. He veered toward the stables and walked up to the open door.

"Anybody home?" he called out cheerfully, poking his head inside.

Acorn glanced up with bleary eyes. He was dozing lazily on his bed of wood shavings next to Milly, the Tibetan goat. He puffed, half annoyed, half happy to see Jamie, then pulled himself up with a groan.

Jamie watched him shake off the wood shavings and trudge toward him, Milly in tow. He grinned—Acorn was so funny when he was sleepy—he looked like the weight of the world was on his shoulders.

"Did you have a good day?" he asked with a grin.

As an answer, Acorn laid his huge head in his arms and sighed.

Jamie chuckled. It definitely looked like he had: Acorn's eyes were wet and calm, his muscles relaxed—he looked perfectly content.

Jamie was relieved to see his friend so happy. He had felt guilty about spending the whole day away from him and was afraid he had gotten bored, but luckily Milly had come to the rescue. Goats did that to horses. It was the same thing as dogs for people. Acorn and Milly had probably spent their time together, strolling around and lazing about like the two good friends they were.

In theory, Milly was Dillinger's stress reliever and was supposed to keep him company, but she had a mind of her own and couldn't be contained. One day not long ago, she had decided she liked Acorn, so, whenever she fancied, she abandoned her duty and spent some time with him. It was a no-brainer that Acorn was fond of the little horned ball of craziness. Like any Tibetan goat Jamie had ever seen, she was tremendously entertaining and full of quirks, so he could easily imagine Acorn spending the whole day just watching her doing her crazy routines.

"So," he started, and in the cool night of May, he told Acorn about all the exciting things he had done at the river while his friend listened, dozing off in his arms.

7

SLAPPED

The sticky paper ball shot out of the Bic pen like a bullet from a gun. It flew in a straight line through the air, darting past three rows of desks, then splattered on Dan Muldbridge's neck.

Dan scratched instinctively as if bitten by a fly and a thin trail of saliva trickled down his skin. He frowned when he felt the wetness on his hand. As he saw the tiny paper ball stuck on his forefinger, it finally dawned on him. He blushed and spun around.

Three desks behind him, Luka Gassner burst into mocking laughter. Blonde and athletic, he looked like the son of a Greek god and, as such, he seemed to lack any restraint or judgment. His desk mate, Simon Perk, high-fived him in praise of his ace aim.

Dan glanced desperately toward the door, but no teachers or school staff were in sight.

Luka bit off a piece of paper and started chewing, preparing another bullet.

Dan bent down his head sheepishly, resigned to serve as a dartboard.

Jamie watched the scene with a sickening rage swelling up in his stomach. "Stop it!" he called out from his desk on the opposite side of the classroom.

Luka turned. His lips curled down menacingly. "Mind your own business, Blackshear!" he growled, pronouncing his last name as if it were a filthy word. He turned back and loaded the ball of paper into his Bic pen. The people in the rows in front of him shuffled over to avoid getting hit.

Cowards! Jamie thought. He tore a page from his notebook and strode to Dan's desk.

Luka inhaled, then blew hard. The paper bullet shot out of the pen.

Jamie raised the sheet of paper. The spitball splatted on the white surface and dropped onto the desk of Dara Stanton and Elise Wilkins right behind.

"Ewww," squealed them in unison.

"Gross!"

"Take it off!"

Jamie glowered at them. Not only had they done absolutely nothing to help Dan, but they were also acting as if it was his fault they got a spitball on their desk.

Behind him, Dan glanced up nervously.

"Whaddya think you're doing?" Luka barked.

Jamie looked up and saw him kick his chair aside and start toward him. He winced at the idea of being hit, but turned anyway, standing his ground. Luka was bigger and stronger; a punch from him was sure to hurt.

Suddenly Luka stopped in his tracks, throwing an alarmed glance at the door. He pulled his tail between his legs and scampered back to his desk.

Jamie knew immediately who had entered the room. He crushed the paper in his hand and turned around, molding his face into a neutral expression. "Good morning, Ms. Ambrose," he said together with his classmates.

He sat back down at his desk and studied her for clues about her mood. Was it a green or a red day? Ms. Ambrose put down her purse and stared gingerly at a mail slip in her hand, or maybe it was a parking ticket—Jamie couldn't tell—then she pursed her lips and glanced up at the class. Red day, Jamie thought. Incoming.

"Let's see if you have learned your spelling lists."

Jamie saw a malevolent gleam in her eyes—it was clear she was really looking forward to nailing somebody. He turned instinctively toward Dan, who was the usual victim. He had turned sickly pale and was staring at his notebook, obviously afraid that if he looked up, Ms. Ambrose would call on him. She'd get him anyway, Jamie thought, unless a miracle happened. He could only hope Dan would get an easy word.

Ms. Ambrose stood up. "Who wants to spell emergency?"

Jamie was about to raise his hand, when Francesca's voice echoed in his head: We voted. You need to stop. He gritted his teeth. Fine, he thought, if that's what they want...

Sara, next to him, raised her hand.

Ms. Ambrose nodded toward her. "Yes, Sara?"

"E-M-E-R-G-E-N-C-Y."

"Correct."

She didn't care, Jamie thought, but at least she was letting people answer. If the others raised their hands too, maybe everything would be all right after all.

"Knowledge," Ms. Ambrose offered to the class.

Jamie turned to see if anybody was going to answer. They weren't. He frowned. Don't they understand this is just going to make it worse?

Ms. Ambrose turned toward him as she habitually did when noone answered a question.

Jamie glanced at Francesca, who shot him a warning look. He could feel Ms. Ambrose's eyes on him. He knew she expected him to answer, but he couldn't—he had been prohibited from doing that. Prohibited... he repeated to himself with contempt. He had been outnumbered. It wasn't right, nevertheless, if your whole class was against you, what could you do? He looked away.

Ms. Ambrose frowned, then turned around. "Nobody wants to spell knowledge?"

A dead silence swept the classroom.

"Very well..."

Great, Jamie thought, they had just granted her license to kill. They were really asking for it. He glanced quickly over his shoulder: his classmates were all shifting uncomfortably in their seats. It served them right. Let's see how well they did on their own.

"Elizabeth," Ms. Ambrose called out.

Elizabeth Newe, a little chestnut-haired girl, startled. She raised her mousy face and stared at Ms. Ambrose like a deer in a spotlight. She swallowed, then said in almost a whisper, "K-N-O-L-E-D-G-E?"

"Kno-ledge?" Ms. Ambrose mocked. She bore down on Elizabeth and slapped her.

The little girl blushed scarlet.

Ms. Ambrose had found her victim, Jamie thought. At least Dan could breathe for the day. Or so he hoped. Still, he did not like it. They had voted against him, but he gave him no pleasure seeing Elizabeth being slapped. He could have answered all of the spelling questions and nobody would have gotten hurt. Why did it have to go this way?

"K-N-O-W-L-E-D-G-E!" Elizabeth blurted out.

"You're not so stupid after all," Ms. Ambrose said, dripping sarcasm. Then she shot out, "Jamie, spell faucet!"

He gave a start. So that's what she thought? She assumed he wasn't answering because he hadn't studied. Fat chance. And Francesca couldn't tell him not to answer a direct question. "F-A-U-C-E-T." He enunciated each letter with confidence.

Ms. Ambrose's eyebrows raised questioningly.

Jamie saw her squint her eyes, probably wondering what game he was playing. A second later, impatience took over again. She turned toward Dan.

Stupid, Jamie thought to himself. He should have misspelled the word. He should have given her what she wanted. Now she was going to rip Dan apart.

"Dan, would you like to spell potato for us?"

Jamie watched him blink and look up at her—he could never spell that word right. He wished he could beam the answer into Dan's brain by thinking it aloud in his head. He stared at him as he moved his lips, repeating the word silently.

"I am waiting," Ms. Ambrose hissed, cross-armed.

Dan startled, swallowed, mouthed the word a few more times, made some strange signs with his hands, then began, "P..." and looked up for confirmation.

Ms. Ambrose didn't flinch.

Dan hesitated, then whispered, "O-T-A-T..." and stopped again.

Come on, Dan, Jamie thought, you're almost there. O, say O. Say O and you're off the hook!

Dan closed his eyes and said, "O."

Yes! Jamie clutched his fist in victory.

"That's it?" asked Ms. Ambrose.

Jamie felt a wave of dread gripping him.

Dan's eyes widened in terror. He quickly scanned the room in search of the answer.

Jamie met his gaze and nodded imperceptibly.

Dan looked up at Ms. Ambrose and said, "Yes...?"

She pursed her lips as if she had just tasted acid.

Jamie grinned. Dan: 1, Ms. Ambrose: 0.

"Very well, then. Spell definition."

What!? But that's not on today's list, Jamie thought. She wanted Dan to fail at all costs. She let everybody else off the hook after they answered. That wasn't fair. He wanted to raise his hand, but remembered Francesca's order. He looked around, hoping somebody would come to Dan's rescue. Instead, his classmates were all quailing. Cowards! They could do whatever they wanted, but he wasn't going to let Dan in a fix, when he knew the answer. He shot up his hand.

Francesca aimed a scorching look at him.

He glowered back. He didn't care about her prohibition anymore. She and everybody else could stuff it.

Ms. Ambrose noticed their movements and turned around. Her eyes became two slits. "I didn't ask you, Jamie. Lower your hand."

"But I know the answer!"

"And I said I didn't ask you, Blackshear."

He winced at being addressed so formally. He knew it was a warning. He thought of lowering his hand, but couldn't. "But Dan already answered the other question."

Ms. Ambrose turned back as if he had not spoken.

"Are you going to answer?" she asked Dan. "Or do you prefer an F on your report card?"

Dan started shaking as big drops of sweat trickled down the back of his neck, then he mumbled, "D... I—"

"I?" Ms. Ambrose laughed. "I? Where did you see an I, Dan?" Without warning, she slapped him hard. "Think!"

Jamie couldn't take it anymore. "E!" he blurted out. "It's an E, not an I!"

Ms. Ambrose wheeled around and grabbed him by the ear.

Jamie heard a crack near his lobe, then a wave of heat

invaded the right side of his face. He yelped in pain as she lifted him to his feet.

"Go to the corner!" she bellowed, pulling him toward the end of the classroom.

"It's not fair," Jamie repeated aimlessly, his head jammed by pain. "He already answered a question!"

"Mind your own business, Blackshear! To the corner!"

"For what? I didn't do anything!"

"For being a know-it-all and an idiot!" Ms. Ambrose shouted as she kicked him hard.

Knocked off balance, he hurtled toward the wall. He threw out his arms just in time and stopped himself in the corner. Blushing and shaking, he massaged his ear and peeked over his shoulder.

Ms. Ambrose swooped down on Dan like a vulture. "D-E, and what?" she barked.

He had just made things worse, Jamie thought. Stupid, stupid, stupid! Ms. Ambrose was going to eat him alive.

Dan was now a sickly shade of violet and it looked like he was about to throw up. He tried to speak, but stuttered, "F-f-f...," then stopped, confused.

Ms. Ambrose slapped him again. "Think!"

Dan startled as if hit by a bolt of lightning. "F-double F-I-N-I-T-I-O-N!" he screamed out in panic.

"Double f?" growled Ms. Ambrose. She raised her arm and came down hard from behind, hitting him right above the neck.

Dan's head shot forward in an arc. A crack echoed as he slammed face-first against his own desk and bounced back. He raised his hands to his forehead and started crying in pain.

"Why are you so stupid, eh!? You're a shame to your parents!" Ms. Ambrose looked down at him for a moment, then strode back to her chair.

Jamie turned around before she could unleash more punishment. The image of Dan's head bouncing against his own desk burnt bright before his eyes. Dan's sobs echoed in the silent room, punctuated by the clicking of Ms. Ambrose's heels on the floor. She had hit him before, but this was awful. Jamie's stomach became a hurtful knot as a wave of panic washed over him. He didn't want to be beaten, he didn't want to be next. He should have minded his own business. He should have let her do what she wanted.

Behind him, he heard her say, "I don't think you want your parents to know that you can't spell."

He turned slightly and looked at her reflection in the window: she was sitting at her desk, looking at the class as if nothing had happened. She adjusted her hair and continued, "So it's better if you don't go home crying for nothing. They won't believe you anyway—they know you're lazy."

He realized Ms. Ambrose wasn't just talking to Dan—she was addressing the whole class. She put on her glasses and scratched something in the book register. Probably their grades, Jamie thought. Another wave of panic gripped him—he was getting a bad grade, maybe even a note. He had never gotten a note before. His father wouldn't like it; he wouldn't like it at all.

"These things are between us and need to stay between us," Ms. Ambrose continued before looking up from the register. "And you better not go around telling tales to people. I'm your teacher. Everything I do is for your own good. You better be grateful, because I'm not doing anything wrong. But if you tell your moms, I won't be able to give you good grades anymore."

Why did she have to say that every time? He didn't want bad grades! He wasn't going to say anything—he never did. His blood chilled at the idea of what his father would do if he got bad grades.

"They know," she said softly. "I'm just doing what they asked me to and you'd be really ungrateful children to go and complain to them. Your parents want you to behave, they want you to be good at school, so don't go bother them. You'll just upset them. Be good children and listen to your teacher."

Had he not been good? thought Jamie. He had never been hit before, but now she was calling him an idiot and a know-it-all. Was he? Was he an idiot? Ms. Ambrose was their teacher, she knew... He had just tried to help Dan. It wasn't fair how she had treated him— she hit him. Dan had already answered and she hit him so hard his head bounced against the desk. That was wrong, wasn't it? And Mom wanted them to be treated this way? Really? Was he being ungrateful? Was Ms. Ambrose going to flunk him because he had been bad? Was he going to fail school now? Could she do that?

He turned and stared back at the wall, dazed.

When he looked up, Jamie felt as if a bubble around him had suddenly burst. A rush of sound and movement overwhelmed him as kids poured by at his sides and ran up to their parents. He found himself standing outside the school gate, not sure how he had gotten there. It seemed as if a hole had swallowed time. He cast about for his mom—she was waving at him from across the street. He headed toward her.

The image of Dan's head bouncing against his desk flashed again in front of Jamie's eyes. It was so mean, so... so evil! Evil? That's what Ms. Ambrose was? But she was their teacher and he was an idiot... He shook his head, trying to make the thought go away.

He got in the car and threw his backpack on the backseat. He sat staring straight ahead absentmindedly as the school glided out of sight. Suddenly he realized his mom was studying him.

"Jamie, are you OK?"

They know. They asked me to do it, Ms. Ambrose's voice echoed in his mind. Don't go bother them. He nodded, forcing a smile.

Maddie frowned. "What's wrong, kitten?"

Dan's head bounced hard on the desk before his eyes. He had never seen anything like that—it must hurt like crazy. He suddenly felt the urge to tell her everything. She couldn't have possibly asked Ms. Ambrose to do something so awful—she was his mom!

"I'm an idiot too. I'll catch it now like everybody else," he blurted. That's not what he wanted to say, but that's what came out. He wasn't even aware he was so scared until he said it aloud. He was terrified. He didn't want to be hit like Dan; he didn't want Dan to be hit again. It was wrong.

He turned and saw Maddie frowning deeply. Panic seized him. Don't go and complain. Be good children and listen to your teacher, Ms. Ambrose had always said. Was his mom going to be mad at him for complaining?

Maddie studied him, then said in a controlled, soothing voice, "What do you mean? What happened, honey?"

She was listening, Jamie thought. She wasn't angry—she didn't look angry. "Ms. Ambrose slapped me," he said all at once. "She said I'm an idiot and a know-it-all." He felt tears welling up in his eyes, but he fought them back. "She hit Dan. She slammed his head against his desk and she kicked me. She slapped Elizabeth too. She slaps them all the time. She hates Dan. She hits Dan, Elizabeth, Beth, David and Nick the most, but the others too. She never hit me, because I always got good grades. But now I'm an idiot too. I'll catch it too. And Dan, she hurt him so much, he was crying. I heard his head crack against the desk." He caught his breath, then continued, "I don't want to catch it too. Mom, am I an idiot?" He didn't know why he was telling her all that. He had kept the secret for so long—it just all came flooding out of him.

Maddie looked stunned. "What...? No, you're not." She

seemed to gather her thoughts, then asked, "Has she done this before?"

"Yes, of course," he answered mechanically.

"Of course? What do you mean, of course?"

Didn't she know? He frowned, confused.

Maddie rounded on him, her grip on the wheel tightening. "Since when, Jamie?"

He snapped out of his thoughts. "I don't know... She's always done it. As soon she started teaching us... After a month, maybe. I'm not sure."

"Since third grade!?" Maddie shot him a reproachful look. "Why didn't you tell me before?"

Jamie flinched. Ms. Ambrose told him not to. She was his teacher, so... "Ms. Ambrose told us it was something between us. She always said she wasn't doing anything wrong and that she would give us bad grades if we told our parents, because you knew and you had asked her to do it and we were just being ungrateful if we told you."

"I told her to do what!?" Maddie swore loudly.

Jamie startled. He had never heard his mother swear before.

Maddie spun around. "I never told your teacher to do anything like that, Jamie," she said forcefully, then turned back, glaring at the road ahead. "And if I had ever seen her lay a hand on you, I would have ripped her arms off!"

Jamie's eyes widened at the sight of how furious his mom was. He believed her and wished she had been there when it first happened. He wished she could have protected him then.

Maddie cursed at Ms. Ambrose again, then she pulled over at the side of the road. She let go of the steering wheel and turned to look at Jamie in the eyes. "Never, ever again trust somebody who tells you not to tell me something, Jamie. Understand? When they do that, they are lying to you. You should come straight to me and tell me, because these people are trying to hurt you. Do you understand?"

He nodded.

"Promise me!"

"I promise," he said mechanically, but he was thinking about what she had just said. So Ms. Ambrose had actually lied to him. She was their teacher—why did she do that? She wanted to hurt him? Why?

"What a piece of scum!" Maddie hissed, gritting her teeth. "This is unacceptable! I am going to talk to the class representative, to the principal if I need to. The hag must be fired!"

Fired, Jamie repeated in his head, and the thought flooded him with relief. It would be wonderful to not have Ms. Ambrose as a teacher anymore. His mom really believed him if she wanted to get Ms. Ambrose fired. He felt a rush of gratitude filling his chest.

"What she did is wrong, Jamie, and you did the right thing in telling me, you understand? It's not between you and her. She can't hit kids. It's abuse—it's against the law. She lied to you. She is a bad person, you understand? You're not an idiot, baby. You are a brave boy."

He nodded quickly, even if he could barely take in all she was saying. He didn't feel brave. He was scared and felt bad that he was even more scared for himself than for Dan. But he couldn't help it. It was true, why had he not spoken before? Dan had been hit all this time. He wasn't brave, he was a coward! He should have told his mom when it all started. He felt dirty. He felt as if he had done something against his will. He felt wrong, wronged, cheated, duped. A burst of hatred exploded in him at the thought of what Ms. Ambrose had made him do. Never, never again, he swore to himself. Never! He was right about her —Ms. Ambrose was evil.

Maddie caressed him. "Everything will be all right, baby. Don't worry."

Jamie felt a heavy weight lift off, but doubt nagged at him. Could his mom really get Ms. Ambrose fired? That would be great.

Maddie put her hands on the steering wheel, then turned back again. "Let's not say anything to Dad for now, OK?"

He nodded. No problem. He had no desire to tell his father. He wasn't sure why, but he felt his dad would make fun of him for having been beaten by an old lady. He turned and watched the road glide toward him, wondering what was going to come next.

8

COPING

Jamie felt his father's eyes boring into him. He heard him gulp down some beer, then resume chewing his sandwich slowly, making a deliberate crunching noise. He sensed something was coming and prayed it wasn't about school. He knew he was not going to be able to hide what had happened today if his dad started digging in. He hated to be outsmarted so easily, but his father could always make him say what he wanted to know and he inevitably ended up feeling stupid.

"So, did you get a new girlfriend?" Jan asked point blank. His voice sounded hoarse, as if he had smoked too much, and his breath smelled of beer and ash.

Jamie looked up, a sinking feeling in the pit of his stomach. He shook his head cautiously. Why did his dad ask him that question all the time? Why was it so important that he got a girlfriend?

Jan scoffed. "Not yet? What are you waiting for?"

"Jan, leave him alone," cut in Maddie.

"What? I wanna know if my son's gonna turn into a faggot or what."

"Stop it. He's eleven. What do you want him to do?"

"I already had a girlfriend when I was his age. And a job."

Jamie saw Mom repress an answer. It was useless to argue with Dad. He was always right, or he'd find a way to win the argument if you talked to him long enough. He would flip you belly-up like an omelet before you could realize it.

Jan gulped down his beer and finished the last bite of his sandwich. "All right," he exhaled, standing up. He brushed the bread crumbs from his jeans and went to put on his jacket.

Maddie raised her brows. "Are you going out?"

"Meeting up with the boys."

Maddie stiffened. "Remember you have lesson at four. And the rails still need painting, or they'll start rotting again."

"I'll do it tomorrow."

Jamie saw her mom's eyelashes flicker as her expression darkened. She stood up wearily and kissed Jan good-bye. "I need to buy groceries."

He leveled eyes with her. "For what? There's still stuff in the fridge."

Jamie felt the air around them chill. It was always the same excruciating scene whenever Mom asked Dad for money.

"Only for another day. I can't go out to buy one egg at a time, Jan."

He grunted and pulled out a ten dollar bill from his pocket.

"I'll need more than that."

"What for? You gonna buy the whole store?"

"Do you want to eat or what?"

"If your cooking can be called eating."

Maddie winced. "Cook yourself if you don't like it. I've already plenty enough to do."

"What's that supposed to mean!?" Jan snarled back. "That I don't? I'm the one who brings home the bacon here. You'd both be out in the street if it weren't for me."

"Then, give me the money so your child can eat!"

Jamie braced himself, ready for his father to start shouting and insulting them both, but he just narrowed his eyes malevolently and handed Mom another ten dollars.

She glared at him and kept her hand out.

He swore under his breath and passed her another ten dollars, then turned around. He walked up to Jamie and slapped him on the back of his head.

Jamie felt a surge of rage shoot up inside him. It hurt! He made a wrenching effort to remain calm, then made to kiss his dad good-bye.

Jan, instead, pinched his cheek hard.

"Oww!"

Jan chuckled and slapped him away.

Jamie twisted in his seat, now full-on angry. He massaged his cheek and glowered at him. He saw the self-satisfied smirk on his father's face—as if he made a great joke—and felt the urge to slap him back. Why did he have to hurt him to be affectionate? Why couldn't he be gentle for once? It seemed he enjoyed hurting him.

"Bye, chicken," he said, and walked away.

Jamie glared at his back, resisting the urge to throw something at him. At that moment, he caught sight of his boots—they were shining new. Jamie clenched his jaws until he heard his teeth grind. He wanted to punch his father. So, there wasn't enough money to buy food, but he had enough to buy himself a pair of new boots!? And he didn't need them—the ones he had were perfectly fine. If someone needed new shoes or clothes, that was Mom. He felt a surge of searing rage. That wasn't fair. It wasn't right!

He watched his father walk outside, followed by Mom. He heard them exchange another couple of unintelligible words, then the door of the car slammed shut. The engine turned on and the rustling of the wheels on the ground faded away quickly.

Maddie walked back in. She went straight to the kitchen sink and started washing the dishes in silence.

Jamie played with some bread crumbs, wasting time. He didn't want to be alone right now.

"Do you want some dessert?" she asked abruptly.

Jamie looked up. Mom was beaming at him from the sink. Her sudden change of mood startled him, but he was glad she was making an effort to cheer him up. He nodded.

Maddie tapped her index finger on her chin. "I was thinking some banana, a few nuts and honey. What do you say?"

"Mm-hmm," he replied with a shrug.

"Is that a yummy sound I hear?"

Jamie could not repress a smile.

"Hmm, hmm!" Maddie boomed in a fake monster voice, "Me like desserrrt!" She growled and stomped forward.

Jamie raised his arms, ready to ward off the storm of smooches that was probably coming.

"Me liiike..." Maddie paused for effect, scowling with crazed eyes.

Jamie giggled, unable to keep a straight face.

"Tickles!" she shouted and shot down, tickling him mercilessly.

He squirmed around like an eel, overcome by a fit of giggles.

"Tickle, tickle, tickle!" she chanted like a mad torturer.

"I surrender, I surrender!"

Maddie let go of him.

Jamie sat back and took a big breath.

"Aaahh!" she mocked him.

"It's not fair. I wasn't ready!"

"Are you ready now?" she replied, advancing.

"No, no, no!" Jamie threw up his hands. "If I laugh more, I'm gonna pee in my pants!"

"Ha!" Maddie pulled back and wiped her nose with her hand like a street thug. "Better watch out, kiddo. No messing with the Ticklelator!"

They both burst into laughter at her bad joke.

Maddie caressed him. "So, ready for some cheap dessert, tiger?"

"Yesss!"

She nodded and went to the kitchen counter.

Jamie glanced at the remains of the apple pie. "You don't need to make me something from scratch, Mom. I can eat the leftovers."

"Don't worry, kitten. I'll whip you up something quick."

He smiled. Mom always tried to make the most of what she had. He thought it was creative and smart of her. Instead of pining for what they didn't have, she managed to make things that sometimes were even better than what was sold at the store.

Maddie opened the cupboard and picked up a small glass spice bottle. "And I think today we'll sprinkle it with some cinnamon," she said, winking at Jamie, "just for kicks!"

Jamie nodded, smiling in anticipation. He was always up for something new. Even if it turned out not to taste that great, trying a new food or a new combination always appealed to him. It was an adventure and he liked adventures in whatever form they came. Only the brave dare, he thought proudly.

He watched her concoct the handmade dessert with a few quick touches. When she was finished, she scooped it into a nice colorful bowl, picked up his favorite red spoon and laid everything neatly in front of him.

"Enjoy."

Jamie waited while she poured some coffee for herself. He studied the golden and brown glob in front of him and decided it looked great—it resembled a gooey alien brain or a really cool space jellyfish that had beached in his bowl. Actually, better not a jellyfish, he thought. It would probably taste like Jell-O and he didn't like that.

Maddie sat down and raised her steaming mug.

Jamie raised his bowl.

"Cheers!" they said in unison.

He took a spoonful of dessert and gave it his professional taster treatment. He let it sit on his tongue to make the flavors seep in, then chewed slowly in order to mix the aromas by slow degrees. Mom's treat was as good as always. It was sweet and crunchy because of the nuts, squishy because of the banana, plus the cinnamon added a nice kick and a tiny bit of powdery texture to the whole. It was good, really good. Worth a nine in his Master Book of Desserts My Mom Makes.

"Is it all right?"

Jamie nodded. "Love it! The cinnamon's great too."

"Good!" She smiled and relaxed back in the chair.

They ate in silence, enjoying each other's company.

Jamie loved these moments. The simple act of sitting next to his mom felt wonderful. It was the same as with Acorn: they didn't need words, just to be in each other's presence. Unfortunately, these happy breaks never lasted. Soon enough, in fact, the anxiety of what had happened crept back between them.

Maddie was the first to break the silence. "This morning I got sidetracked by some errands and didn't finish the boxes. Do you want to help me out?"

"Sure." He still didn't want to be alone, plus some movement would keep his brain busy for a while. He hoped he would sweat too—it always made him feel better. It was as if bad thoughts poured out of his skin together with drops of perspiration.

"Let's do it then!" Maddie exclaimed, slamming her fist against the table.

Jamie smiled and jumped up.

They put on their jackets and headed through the stables. When they arrived at the toolshed, they picked up a wheelbarrow and fork each.

Jamie felt the combined weight of the tools pulling down at his shoulders—he was always surprised by how hefty they were. Both instruments were blunt, ponderous objects that weren't meant to be pretty, but to do the job and last. He liked that. He took comfort in holding them, in feeling they had been around for years, always digging and carrying dirt, yet still full of the dignity of their purpose.

"Do Dillinger and Dexter," Maddie said. "I'll take the rest, OK?"

"Cool." Jamie drove to the left side of the stables and parked the wheelbarrow next to Dillinger's box. As soon as he pulled the large iron handle of the door, Milly shot toward him, horns first.

He jumped back. "Hey!"

Milly darted past him, skidded into the hallway like a miniature hairy panzer, then clip-clopped out of the stables.

Dillinger made a start for her.

Jamie blocked him. "No, no, no! One out is enough!" He shoved him back and pulled the wheelbarrow in front of the door.

Dillinger shot him a dirty look, snorted and showed him his buttocks.

"Oh, come on, Dill."

"Are you OK?" Maddie called from the opposite box.

"Yeah, just Milly, the master of escape. She thinks she's in Alcatraz or something."

Maddie chuckled.

He picked up the fork and started flipping the wood shavings. He glanced up at Dillinger, still sulking in the corner. "I'm sorry, Dill, OK? I didn't do it on purpose, I swear. I just forgot you live with a psycho goat."

Dillinger turned slightly, studying him.

Jamie knew that he was listening, so he went on, "Don't worry, OK? I'll bring her back." At that moment, the fork drove into something solid. He pulled up—it was heavy—and flipped the fork. A mass of wet shavings congealed by the horse's pee landed flat on the bedding—a 'pee cake', as he referred to it. He picked it up with the fork and threw it into the wheelbarrow.

It was actually pretty clever, he mused. Somebody somehow figured out that wood shavings would cake up like that when wet, so they decided to use it as horse bedding to make their life easier. How they came up with it, he really couldn't fathom. I mean, why use wood shavings as horse bedding in the first place? They weren't exactly your first choice. Were there people, like scientists, who just sat down and thought this stuff through, then started making experiments? So weird...

Jamie shook his head and started working in earnest, losing himself in the physical toil.

Forty minutes later, when he finished, he was sweaty and aching. His back was tight, his arms tired and his hands raw. He felt much better though. His mind was clearer—all the manual labor had burned away some of his anxiety.

He started wondering what he would do next. He could go out with Acorn. That would certainly be a nice way to spend his afternoon. He had homework, but that could wait until evening. He felt he needed to talk to somebody about what had happened, though. So that's what he wanted, he realized. He felt let down that he didn't want to be around Acorn more. He had already abandoned him the day before to go out with Dan, so it wasn't fair to keep him at home again today. He was also sure that with Acorn he'd have a good time, whereas with somebody else he could never tell. Nevertheless, he had the urge to speak to someone right now. He would make it up to Acorn later.

Maybe he should check on Dan, he thought. He felt awkward calling him, but it was probably the right thing to do.

Maddie finished cleaning the last box. She put down the wheelbarrow with a tired sigh and raised her hand. "Well done, buddy!"

They high-fived, then unloaded the wheelbarrow on the manure pile in the back of the house and put the tools back in their place.

"I am going to school to talk to some people," Maddie told him as they were walking back. "Everything will be all right, OK?"

Jamie nodded. That was great news. She was moving quickly. He felt hopeful.

"You're going out with Acorn today?"

"Yeah, maybe"

"Be careful, OK? And don't come back late."

"OK." Mom always worried too much. Nevertheless, he secretly liked it. It reminded him every time that she really loved him. He wasn't going to tell her though, otherwise she'd probably go overboard with it.

He went upstairs and waited until she got changed. When he finally heard the car driving away, he ran downstairs, picked up the phone and dialed Dan's number.

"Hello?" Dan answered on the other line.

Jamie had expected Dan's mom to answer the phone, so he was taken off guard. "Oh... Hey... Hi Dan. It's Jamie."

"...Hi."

"Hi..." This was even more awkward than he had imagined. "Are... Are you all right?"

"Sure, I'm fine. Why?"

His reply left him speechless. Dan was all right? He blanked out. "Uhh... Do you want to do something today?"

"No, I'm going out with my mom."

"Ah, OK."

"Bye."

"Bye, then."

Jamie put down the receiver. He felt queasy. Dan's tone troubled him, but he couldn't pinpoint why. The whole conversation had been really weird. Dan said he was all right, but how could he? Was he too embarrassed to talk? Or maybe he didn't want to disobey Ms. Ambrose? But she had only said not to tell their parents—they could still talk to each other. If Dan didn't want to, though, there was nothing he could do. He, however, did need to talk things over. Who else could he call? Holly, maybe? She was still his friend, after all.

He picked up the phone and dialed.

"Hello," Mrs. Roeg's voice called out on the other end of the line.

A smile cracked on Jamie's face. "Hello Mrs. Roeg. It's Jamie."

"Hello, dear."

"Is Holly home?"

"No, sorry. She's at Francesca's."

He felt his heart plunge. "Oh... OK. It doesn't matter."

"I can give you her number."

"Oh, no, no, thanks."

"Hmm... Is everything all right, Jamie?"

He winced. "Yeah. It doesn't matter, really," he said trying to sound convincing. He hated having to lie to her—she was always so nice to him.

"OK..."

"Thank you, Mrs. Roeg. Have a good day."

"You too, dear. Bye."

He hung up. Great. So now he was back where he had

started. The urge to reach out flared up inside him. He remembered that he had heard Alex, one of his classmate, saying that today he and his friends were going to play soccer. He wasn't super fond of Alex because he could be nasty when he was in a bad mood, but they had been friends—they used to play sports together all the time. He hoped today was a good day. He needed it to.

He run upstairs and got changed. He put on sweatpants and hoodie and ran back down.

Before leaving, he checked on Acorn to say bye. He was in the school while a couple of the other horses were grazing in the paddock.

As soon as he saw him, Acorn trotted up to the fence, trailed by Milly.

Jamie slapped his forehead in frustration a the sight of the goat. He had promised Dillinger to bring Milly back, but had completely forgotten about it. The old horse was going to hate him.

Acorn stepped forward and pushed his head against Jamie's chest. He wanted to be petted.

Jamie rubbed him under his chin. The warmth of Acorn's skin and the rhythmic puffs of his breath against his ribs infused him with a happy calmness.

"I know you want to go out, buddy, but I've got something to do. Tomorrow, I promise, we'll go for a nice walk, OK? Have fun in the sun and don't hurt yourself!" He sounded like his mom.

He gave Acorn a last pat, then turned to Milly. "You instead. You come with me." He got hold of the collar around the goat's skinny neck and steered her out of the paddock. She offered surprisingly little resistance.

Acorn was not as well disposed and snorted loudly in disapproval.

"I know, I know," Jamie apologized. "I'm really mean today, but I promised, buddy. I've got to do this."

Acorn didn't want to hear reason. He pulled back his ears and bared his teeth, intimating a bite.

"Hey! Don't you even think of that! You got me!?"

Acorn shook his head and bolted away, sulking.

9

TIME BETTER SPENT

After securing Milly with Dillinger, Jamie jumped on his bike.

He pedaled quickly past the patch of woods behind the farmstead and passed the spread of sparse houses that preceded the soccer field. His old kindergarten came into view. He liked the place, even if it was a nondescript block of cement, because it had a nice persimmon tree in the back with branches that stretched beyond the high wall. He loved persimmons, so he always kept a close watch on the tree during picking season and took his chance to steal some every time he was sure not to get caught.

He passed the kindergarten, a house gated with tall pine trees and finally he spotted the parking lot next to the soccer field. Alex was already there, thick in conversation with his friends.

Jamie slowed down. He hadn't given much thought to the possibility of not being able to talk to Alex alone. He didn't really know his friends and the few times he had seen them around, they hadn't seemed too friendly. He had no choice now, though. It would have looked weird if he asked Alex to come talk to him alone. He'd have to try and find the right moment to drop the question. Or perhaps he would actually like his friends once he got to know them. Then he could play soccer with them. That would be nice too, he thought. He would have loved to have new friends.

He biked to the far corner of the parking lot where the group was gathered. Besides Alex, there were another four boys the same age. One was Marc Parnell, blonde and sturdy. The other was Alfred "Alf" Dickson, a tall redhead who had the body of a boy three years older. Jamie didn't know the other two.

As he approached, he noticed that the five boys were all fanned out around an older kid, maybe fifteen or sixteen years old, who was sitting on his motorbike. Jamie didn't know him, but he had often seen him with Alex and his company. The boy looked cool wearing a dark leather jacket the same color as his hair. The others around him were listening intently to what must be a good story.

They all turned as he drew up to them. Jamie felt something like an invisible barrier between him and the group. It felt as if they were enclosed in a bubble and he shouldn't have entered that space. It was too late to turn back, though.

"Hi, Alex," he said, pulling up next to him and hoping that if the other boys saw that he knew Alex, they'd accept him in their circle.

Alex nodded laconically and turned around.

Jamie was taken aback. He glanced quickly toward Marc and Alf, waving at them. "Hey!"

Marc nodded and Alf said automatically, "What's up?"

Jamie shrugged. He never knew how to reply to that.

"Do I know you?" came the voice of the older boy on the motorbike.

Jamie turned and shook his head. "No," he said, then he gathered his courage and shot out his hand. "I'm Jamie."

The boy shook it, smiling. "Andrew. Wait, you're the kid with the horses, right?"

"Ehm..." Jamie glanced nervously around, afraid that the others would all start making fun of him. "Yeah..."

"Nice place," Andrew said brightly. "My sister takes lessons with your dad. She loves it."

"Cool..." Jamie didn't know what else to say. This Andrew guy was nice, though.

Andrew turned his attention back to Alex and his friends to finish the interrupted conversation. He lit the cigarette he was holding and offered it to them. "So, who wants to try?"

"It's bad for you," Jamie said automatically.

Alex and the other boys shot him a look.

Well, he thought, it was, and it also tasted like crap. He knew that firsthand. When he was four, his father let him try a cigarette. It was just a joke he made to get a laugh in front of his friends, yet the experience had cleared in one stroke all his desire to smoke ever again. The shock and the memory were indelibly burnt in his brain. He could still feel the burning spasm in his lungs, the pain in his throat and the disgusting aftertaste in his mouth. Plus, he hated smoke anyway. His dad always smoked in the car when they traveled. If there was something worse than smoking yourself, it was having to endure somebody else's smoke. It always made him sick and angry because his dad knew he didn't like it, yet he smoked anyway, and in a closed space where he couldn't avoid it.

Alex took the cigarette from Andrew. He placed it between his lips and expertly sucked in. The tobacco burnt red with an enticing crackling sound. Alex closed his eyes, savoring the drag.

His expression took Jamie by surprise. Alex looked as if he was enjoying it. Jamie wondered whether his own memory was accurate. Perhaps smoke had seemed so bad because he was little, but now that he was older, it would actually taste good.

Also, it looked really cool. There was something about holding a cigarette in your hand and puffing smoke out of your mouth that automatically made you look grown up. He couldn't deny it.

Alex passed the cigarette to Marc. Marc studied the little stick of paper and tobacco in his fingers with some apprehension. He fumbled with it, unsure how to hold it correctly, then stuck it between his lips. He inhaled. After a second, he screwed up his face and burst into a fit of coughs, eyes watering.

The other boys laughed out loud.

OK, Jamie thought, that was exactly what he remembered. It had not changed. The haze of coolness immediately cleared from his mind. Probably Alex was just used to it.

Embarrassed, Marc glanced up.

"It's always like that the first time. Don't worry," Andrew said with an encouraging smile.

Alex didn't say anything, but a self-satisfied smirk cut across his face.

As the others handed the cigarette around, Jamie started getting restless. Why were they standing there in a parking lot while cars passed by, spewing smog in their faces? This whole business with smoking looked like a big, fat waste of time to him. He wasn't going to have a chance to talk to Alex this way, so why weren't they playing soccer at least or going on a hike or doing something!?

The cigarette traveled back to Andrew, who offered it to Jamie.

He shook his head. "Aren't we going to play soccer?"

Alf looked him up and down. "You know how to play?"

What was that supposed to mean? Jamie didn't like Alf's tone at all. "Of course," he answered flatly. Anybody could play soccer. That's why everybody played it—because it was easy. It wasn't like horseback riding, where you actually needed a special talent. It was just soccer. "Can you?"

"I'm striker."

"Well, I'm a good goalie. I bet I can stop you."

The other boys burst into laughter.

"We'll see," Alf hissed, looming forward.

"Not today," Alex cut in.

"Why not?" Jamie rounded on him. He immediately regretted it. Why was he so worked up? He sounded crazy. Did he really want to pick a fight with Alf and Alex?

Alex glared at him. "The field's muddy and all. I'm not gonna mess up my new sneakers for a stupid game!"

Jamie fell silent. That was the weirdest thing he had ever heard. Since when did Alex care so much about his sneakers? He glanced down at his shoes, curious to see what was so special about them. Nothing. They looked just like regular sneakers. Way too polished and clean if you asked him. Why buy shoes if you weren't going to use them? What was he saving them for, his wedding? They were just shoes. Who cared if they got dirty?

"You wanna go to Turtle Pond?" he insisted. He wanted to do something. He wanted to get away from there and have a chance to talk.

Marc sneered. "And do what?"

Jamie frowned. "I don't know..." He felt everybody's eyes on him. "There's loads of stuff to do—"

"Yeah, like what?" Alex cut in.

The only thing that popped into Jamie's mind was that time he had come home covered head to toes in mud because he had followed a turtle he liked around the pond to see what kind of life she lived. It had been a memorable day, but he thought that if Alex didn't want to soil his dear sneakers, he would have liked even less hearing about this. At a loss, he turned to Andrew for help.

He extracted the cigarette from between his lips. "The pond's not that bad. You can catch some nice fish."

Thank you, Jamie thought.

"Fishing's boring!" Marc blurted, then caught himself and glanced up at Andrew.

He shrugged, unfazed.

"Yeah," joined in the curly-haired boy Jamie didn't know. "My dad drags me fishing with him once a month and I swear I want to shoot myself every time."

"Nice kicks, by the way," the other stranger told Alex. "Where'd you get'em?"

"Down at the mall."

"Nice!"

Jamie felt the discussion slip out of his hands. The attention of the others shifted away at once as if by a draft.

"Yeah, I know," Alex said, gazing fondly at his sneakers.

"Yo, let's go to the mall," Alf jumped in. "They got some kick-ass new games I saw!"

The other kids groaned in approval.

The mall? Jamie thought. You've got to be kidding me! If there was one place he didn't want to go to, it was the mall. These people really rubbed him the wrong way. He couldn't believe he had given up a nice ride with Acorn for this. He stole a glance at his watch, then up at the sky—there would still be enough light for a while. He definitely knew a better way to spend his time.

He turned to his watch again, staring at it purposefully and pretending something suddenly popped up in his mind. "I got to go," he said aloud to no one in particular.

Alex and his friends turned.

"Forgot something." Forgot something? That was so lame, he couldn't believe it came out of his mouth. Oh, well, he just wanted to get away as quickly as possible. "All right, bye!"

Alex and his friends barely raised their hands. They looked happy he was getting out of the way.

He couldn't blame them—he was happy too. He was only sorry to leave Andrew—he had been really nice. "Bye," he repeated just to him.

Andrew grinned knowingly. "Bye, Jamie."

He wheeled around and pedaled away as fast as possible. What a mess, he thought, as the wind rushed in his ears.

In a few minutes he arrived home. He dropped his bike in the yard and ran upstairs to change.

He slipped into his jodhpurs, then put on his paddock boots and half-chaps. He liked this outfit much more than the formal horseback riding breeches and long boots. He felt more comfortable, more free, and he could feel Acorn better against his legs. He grabbed his helmet and was off.

He shot out of the house and ran toward the school.

As soon as he saw him, Acorn galloped up to the gate, neighing loudly.

He knew, Jamie thought. Acorn could read him from a hundred feet away. "What do you think about a ride to the river, buddy?"

Acorn didn't even let him finish. He bolted back and dashed toward the locked exit gate. Without hesitation, he jumped the fence altogether and galloped straight toward his box, disappearing around the corner.

Jamie burst out laughing. "Somebody is looking forward to getting his hooves wet!"

As he came around the bend, he found Acorn peeking out of his door, his big face lit with anticipation. He laughed again. "Hold that thought, buddy. Be back in a sec!"

He strode through the clubhouse and into the tack room. He picked up saddle and bridle, then marched back outside.

Acorn shook his head impatiently as he saw him emerge from the building.

"Coming. I'm coming!" Jamie hauled the tack to Acorn's box, then grabbed the currycomb.

Acorn pulled his ears back at the sight.

Jamie pushed him inside. "Now stay still if you want to get this over with quickly!"

Acorn looked daggers at him, but endured the grooming with less fuss than usual.

Jamie would normally take his time doing everything properly, but today he rushed through it—they needed to hurry up if they wanted to make the most of the remaining daylight.

When Acorn was finally saddled and ready, Jamie led him out of the box and mounted with a quick jump while he was still walking. Acorn broke off in a light trot.

"Hey, let me at least put my feet in the stirrups, man!"

Acorn turned a deaf ear and broke into a canter.

"Jerk!" Jamie slapped his neck in mock outrage. He slid his other foot through the stirrup and took control.

They headed through the woods and in no time they were on their way to the river.

The silence of the place and the rhythmic, hypnotic rocking of Acorn's body under him brought Jamie's deep thoughts to the surface. He wondered whether his mom had managed to have Ms. Ambrose fired. He really hoped so. The memory of Dan's head bouncing against his desk flashed again in front of his eyes. Dan's grimace of pain, horror and humiliation burned deeper into his soul. There was something really wrong with Ms. Ambrose. She was going to hurt a lot of people if nobody stopped her. He had done the right thing telling his mom, he was sure. His classmates certainly had told their parents too. Probably Dan's parents were there with his mom and they too were asking for Ms. Ambrose to be fired.

Acorn shied suddenly.

Jamie struggled to stay mounted.

Acorn flared his nostrils loudly and broke off at a nervous trot.

Jamie tightened his grip on the reins and glanced around, searching the place for the cause of his fright. He couldn't see anything. He patted Acorn. "It's all right, buddy. There's nothing. It's OK." It was probably just the shadows of some leaves shaking in the wind or the sound of a squirrel rummaging through the undergrowth, he thought.

He made to adjust the reins when he suddenly noticed how tightly his fists were clenched. He sighed, shaking his head. Acorn was right after all. There was indeed something scary around—his own thoughts.

He took a deep breath and made an effort to loosen up. Forget Ms. Ambrose, he told himself; forget Dan. You are with Acorn now, in the woods, everything is all right. As he repeated that in his mind, he felt Acorn's chest relax against his legs. He smiled, satisfied. Horses were really amazing animals. You could never hide your feelings from them. You could fool a man, sometimes even a dog, but you could not fool a horse. If you wanted them to be calm, you needed to be calm yourself. If you were sure you could do something, they'd follow you through fire, but if you were afraid, you could point a gun to their temples and they would not take a single step forward. In order to communicate with them, you always had to look inside yourself. It was tiring, but it was the closest thing to telepathy that he could imagine. That did not mean that horses didn't have their own moods, fears, convictions, and so on. They did, and that made the whole business even more interesting. If you were good and put enough work into it, you could literally fuse with your horse: body, mind and soul.

Jamie led Acorn around a tight bend. The path suddenly opened up into a lush glade. The roar of the nearby river gusted toward them with the wind. The air filled with the smell of algae and running water.

They were close. Jamie loosened the reins and let Acorn take the lead. He wanted him to enjoy their little trip.

Acorn put his head down. He took in big drafts of air through his large nostrils, sniffing like a hound dog, and looked around curiously.

Jamie felt Acorn's body uncoil, his muscles stretch and become more lax. He had surrendered control, so Acorn was letting loose too, swaying his massive body from side to side at every step. He felt as if he was sitting on a slinky.

Acorn walked down to where the path gently sloped toward the riverbank.

The sun was shining through the treetops, casting bright reflections on the running water. The air was still lukewarm, but Jamie could feel the coolness of the river fighting its way up.

He laughed under his breath as Acorn walked cautiously to the edge of the bank and smelled the water. He always had to do a full inspection before wading in, even if every time they entered from the same spot.

Finally convinced that it was safe, Acorn plunged his right hoof into the water, then his left. Jamie felt a shiver of delight run through his body, then a huff come out of his nostrils.

Acorn waded in up to his knees. He walked on sure-footedly until he reached the middle of the river. Then he stopped, apparently satisfied of the spot he had picked. He studied the water briefly, skimmed its surface with his muzzle and splashed it around as if to appraise its consistency. Then he plunged half of his face underwater. He gave a little start and exhaled forcefully. Big bubbles burst out on the surface. He pulled his head out of, flaring his nostrils and shaking his head, apparently thrilled, then plunged his head back in and exhaled again.

Jamie had no idea whether Acorn was scared, excited or

whatever else, but he loved watching him. It filled him with wonder to look at his friend do something that obviously made total sense in his head but was quite mysterious to him. Plus, it was just plain funny. He laughed and patted him affectionately.

Acorn turned around his big, dripping face and nuzzled his foot.

"It never gets old, eh!?" Jamie said, nudging him back with his boot.

Acorn flicked up his ears, then turned back to his water game.

Jamie sat back on the saddle and looked around lazily. The sun had just started setting, slowly bathing the river and the woods nearby in a splendid gold. Backlit, everything looked magical: blue-and-green dragonflies skimmed the surface of the river; a swarm of flies hovered over the water like a constellation of golden drops, breaking and reforming endlessly; and bats dashed through the air like black brushstrokes, quicker than the eye.

Despite everything that had happened, Jamie suddenly felt at peace. The glowing air blew through him, swelling him up and lifting him like a kite.

10

MOM'S REPORT

Jamie enjoyed every single drop of sunset, but when the sun finally disappeared behind the hills, he knew he and Acorn needed to make a move. Soon it would be too dark and dangerous to ride through the woods. Luckily, Acorn was satisfied about their little trip and didn't pose any resistance.

They got back on the path and set out at a trot.

They arrived home just as night was falling. The big lights in the school were on and his dad was teaching to a group of ten adults.

Jamie dismounted at the entrance gate and led Acorn in. A beautiful half moon shone in the sky and the woods all around them rustled with every sigh of the breeze. They slowed down as they stepped on the cement floor before the boxes and fumbled their way in.

Acorn went straight to his drinking bowl. As soon as he was done, he turned around and let out a deep nicker.

Jamie rolled his eyes—he was letting him know he was hungry and it was his duty to feed him. "I know, I know," he said, pushing him aside. "I've got only two hands." He took off Acorn's tack, draped it over the lower door and walked out.

He went into the feed room, grabbed a nice slice of hay, filled up half a measure of oats and hauled everything back.

As he popped out of the stables, Acorn stuck his head out of his box and let out a loud neigh.

"I'm coming, I'm coming! Get inside now!"

Acorn didn't move, too eager to get to his food.

Jamie turned sideways, moving the hay out his reach, and swung out his foot. "Come on, scoot!"

Acorn pulled his ears back and stretched his neck to get a bite.

"If you don't let me in, you won't eat anything, genius. Get out of my way!" He twisted and kicked, then charged into the box.

Acorn retreated with his ears pulled back, then sneaked around him and bit a nice mouthful of hay off the bale.

"Hey! You wanna chop off my hand, you mule!?"

Acorn shot him a look and turned away, chewing covetously.

"Glutton. It'd kill you to wait two more seconds!? Sheesh!" He dropped the hay in the corner and poured the oats into the manger.

As soon as he stepped aside, Acorn plunged his head into the hay.

Jamie slapped him, half annoyed, half amused, and stood there watching him. It had been totally worth it to come back and go on a ride with him.

"Thanks, buddy." He hugged Acorns' neck, then crossed under him and walked out of the box. "Good night. See you tomorrow, OK?"

Acorn was apparently too busy hearing the sound of his own chewing to turn around and say good-bye.

Jamie shook his head, then picked up the saddle and bridle and locked the box.

He went to the clubhouse, switched the lights on and walked

into the tack room. He put Acorn's tack on their respective hangers, then walked back to the stables, locked the door and finally strode out into the garden. Thelma was in the driveway. The light in the kitchen was on and a warm smell drifted out of the open door. He sniffed the air and smiled in anticipation.

"I'm back," he said as he walked in.

Maddie, busy washing dishes in the sink, turned around, frowning. "I was starting to worry. Where have you been?"

"I just went with Acorn to the river." He grinned and sat down. "You should have seen him."

She shook her head. "Don't come back so late, OK? It's dangerous."

"I know. I wasn't planning to. I left as soon as the sun went down."

Maddie sighed and relaxed. "Did you have fun?"

"Oh yeah, and Acorn too. You should have been there. He was plunging his head underwater and puffing and thrashing around in the bubbles. He was really funny."

She smiled and dried her hands, glanced at the oven, lost in thought, then seemed to make up her mind and sat down in front of him. "Remember I told you I was going to talk to some people at school, right?"

Jamie nodded. He wanted to hear about that. He really hoped that his mom had managed to get Ms. Ambrose fired.

"So, first I went to see the class rep, Mrs. Winters, Sara's mom."

He nodded. He had never seen Sara's mom. He didn't know she was the class representative. That seemed cool, though. Sara was very smart, so her mom probably was too.

"I told her you came out of school in a state, that you were deeply agitated, and I explained what you told me.

"She listened to me without uttering a word, then said: Oh yes, I know. My daughter has been telling me, but Ms. Ambrose would never do such things. I'm sure it's just rumors. You know kids... You need to take what they say with a grain of salt. After all, they're just kids. They have their own fantasies; they see things the way they want to. They have their sympathies and antipathies... Maybe that day the child hadn't studied and comes up with an excuse. The teacher gives him a flick on the head and the child gets angry, so he makes up a huge story in revenge. You know how these things go."

"I didn't make up any story," cut in Jamie. "Why did she say that?"

"Because she's stupid," Maddie said flatly. "I was already getting angry listening to all her platitudes, but I kept myself in check and said calmly: No, I don't think so. First of all, Jamie has always done well in school—and he's still doing well. Second, I know him and I've never seen him go through a crisis like this. Plus, he told me things in great detail. I'm positive he's telling the truth.

"As an answer, dear Mrs. Winters looked at me smugly and said: Ms. Ambrose never touched my daughter."

Of course she didn't, Jamie thought. She's the best in class. Why would she?

"Really? I told her. So, as long as Ms. Ambrose doesn't touch your daughter, it's all fine? Didn't you just say that she told you what happened? She's the top of the class, isn't she? She's never failed a test, right? So, it's impossible that she'd tell you a story out of spite. Even more because the teacher uses intimidation to shut the children's mouths. So, why would she speak out?

"As an answer, Mrs. Winters let out this odious mocking whimper of a laugh—I just wanted to punch her in the face— and said: Surely you're painting her to be a monster. She's just a teacher, what can she do?"

Why was she defending Ms. Ambrose? Jamie thought angrily. What was wrong with her!?

Maddie sneered. "What can Ms. Ambrose do? I asked my son why he never spoke out and he replied that it was because Ms. Ambrose had repeated to the whole class over and over that what happened at school was something 'between them' and it must stay so. And she told them that if they talked to their moms, then she wouldn't be able to give them good grades anymore. And that they were being ungrateful children. How's that for manipulation, Mrs. Winters?

"Sure, sure—she replied condescendingly—Far from me to doubt what you're saying. It might very well be true, but I can't do anything without any real proof.

"More proof than having your daughter tell you? What more do you want?

"Proof! She didn't need any proof! She was just too comfortable with her little class rep badge and didn't want to rock the boat."

Jamie blinked. He was starting to feel dizzy. It was all wrong.

"If you want proof, I told her, all you need to do is take the children one by one, maybe in the presence of their mothers, who know them best—they'll know whether or not the child is telling the truth.

"The idea of actually doing her job didn't suit her, because she shot a look at me, affronted and said, Oh no, no, this is too much. I really don't feel comfortable. Ms. Ambrose and I both go to the same parish. Our husbands know each other. That would be really inconvenient. I don't want to create a case out of nothing. After all, it wasn't such a big deal."

"What!? Dan got his head smashed against a table!" Jamie almost shouted. That was a big deal!

Maddie nodded. "That's what I told her: First of all, I educate my son, not Ms. Ambrose, I said. So, if he does something wrong, she should come and tell me and I'll take care of it. Second, this is a big deal. Here we're talking about gratuitous violence every day. And to what end, Mrs. Winters? Just for personal, professional gain, in order to appear the best teacher in the district.

"I don't really want to take sides, she replied.

"Excuse me, but aren't you the class rep!? I almost shouted in her face. Why did you take the job then? Just to brag?"

Right, Jamie thought.

"She flashed a dirty look at me. Well, she said: I can't really do anything, but if you want to do something, please do and keep me updated.

"Hypocrite! I started walking away, but I couldn't stand her stupid smugness anymore, so I turned around and said: Anyway, don't lull yourself too much in your security, my dear. Don't you think for a second that your daughter is safe from your friend, because a pig like that, if she pleases, she'll take it out on your child too. And I left."

The silence brought Jamie back to his senses. His head was spinning. That whole conversation didn't make any sense—it was so absurd. Why didn't she believe him? He was telling the truth.

"Since she didn't want to help us," Maddie resumed, "I thought I'd get the other moms together and make the case myself to the principal. I thought I'd go to Dan's mother first, since you told me he was the one who got beaten the most."

Jamie nodded. Dan's mom must be against that. There was no way she could defend Ms. Ambrose after what Dan must have told her. He collected himself and tried to focus again.

"So," Maddie went on, "I got to Dan's house and I told his mother: I don't know if you know that the teacher does this and that, and I know that your son gets hit. I didn't tell her he was the one who was getting beaten all the time."

Jamie frowned. Why didn't she tell her? She should have. It was important.

"But, as soon as I started telling her these things, she just looked down at me. She was very wary of me—you know those very ignorant people who can't seem to understand a situation, who you are, what you want?"

Jamie nodded, but he had only a vague idea of what she meant.

"She was like: who is this woman? What is she doing? What does she want? As if I had a hidden purpose. I kept on going anyway, hoping she'd understand.

"I already went to the class rep, I said, but she's too concerned about keeping her little throne instead of doing her job. Since Jamie told me the names of many of the kids who get hit, I thought I should let the other moms know what is going on. And I wanted to know if you wanted to get together and talk to the principal.

"She looked at me suspiciously as if I were a street vendor who had finally come to the point, and said: Oh, yeah, I know, I know. My son told me he gets scolded sometimes, but it's no big deal. Dan is lazy, he needs a good thrashing every once in a while to get his head straight. Children need to learn about authority."

Jamie was taken aback. How could she say something like that!?

"Dan had come home crying or something," Maddie said. "Yet, seeing her son like that didn't ring any alarm in this woman's brain. She must either be very stupid or she was used to being beaten herself. Maybe when she was little she got thrashed all the time and now she thought it was OK."

Jamie frowned. Was that how it worked?

"And you know—she went on—all the moms together like that. Isn't it too much? To make such a fuss of such a small thing? I'll just get the teacher against me; I'll get in trouble for nothing. I'm sure they're just laying it on thick. They're kids; they lie all the time. It'll pass."

Why did they all think he was lying? Jamie wondered in bewilderment.

"So, she too preferred not to rock the boat," Maddie continued. "All right then, I said, if you're not interested... I thought you didn't know and I just wanted to make sure—

"Oh no, I know—she cut in—I talked to Ms. Ambrose and she assured me Dan was blowing things out of proportion."

Maddie shook her head. "And you believed her?

"Why shouldn't I? She has a reputation. She's not like me and you. Who are you to say she lies? Maybe once or twice she gave Dan a flick on the head to wake him up. So what? If he was being lazy and didn't pay attention in class, he deserved it."

He didn't deserve to have his head smashed against the table, Jamie thought angrily.

Maddie massaged her temples, frustrated. "I couldn't believe what came out of this woman's mouth. She still hit your son, I said. She waved my comment away.

"Dan is such a crybaby. He needs to learn to man up!

"So, she probably hit him too to make him 'man up'. Great. After that gem of wisdom, I left."

Maddie looked Jamie in the eyes. "You did see Dan's head hit the desk, right?"

He nodded, confused. Yes, he did. At least he thought he did. At this point, he was starting not to be sure about anything anymore. It all seemed like a bad nightmare.

"Anyway," she added, "don't worry, OK? I just wanted you to know. It's better if you know."

"Wait, what about Mrs. Roeg and Holly? You didn't go to talk to them too?" Mrs. Roeg would believe him, Jamie was sure. And Holly had seen everything. They would be on his side.

Maddie's expression sagged. "Yes, I did go to Michelle, but she can't help us."

"Why?" Jamie asked slowly, bracing himself.

Maddie hesitated. "I told her what happened and she believed me, but when she tried to talk to Holly, she threw a fit and called you a liar."

Jamie felt his stomach turn over.

"If Holly doesn't talk, there's not much Michelle can do. She said she'll try again as soon as she calms down. I'm sure she's just upset," she added quickly, "and for sure she's intimidated by what Ms. Ambrose has told you all this time. I'm sure she's on your side—you're good friends."

Were, corrected Jamie in his mind. Holly didn't seem to be his good friend anymore.

Maddie took his hand. "I'm sorry. I know it hurts, but we'll figure it out. OK?"

He nodded, but felt like he had preferred not to know about her conversation with Sara's and Dan's moms. He had been very happy a few minutes ago and now he felt miserable. He wished he had gone straight to bed instead of talking to Mom. Now there was a sticky, dark sensation trapped inside him that he did not know how to get rid of.

As soon as he finished his dinner, he climbed up to his room and changed into his pajamas. He wanted this awful day to end as soon as possible. He wished sleep would erase the pain and confusion he felt. Perhaps, if he forgot, things would be better. Perhaps tomorrow would be better; things could change.

Sleep did not come, though. Jamie lay in his bed for almost an hour, his head spinning from one event to the other, revisiting his morning and the conversation with his mom in great detail, faces and words flashing behind his closed eyelids.

Finally, he opened his eyes, surrendering to the notion that he wasn't going to fall asleep anytime soon.

He sat up in bed and wondered how he could get himself tired enough. He couldn't go for a bike ride in the middle of the night. Nor could he play outside. He didn't feel like watching TV or reading a book either. He just wanted to sleep! Why couldn't he!?

His stomach hurt. Not knowing exactly what he was going to do, he put on a hoodie and walked downstairs. He shuffled into the kitchen and grabbed a piece of bread. He hoped it would act as a sponge and absorb some of the acidity he was feeling.

Trying not to make too much noise, he grabbed the keys and unlocked the door.

He stepped outside into the clear night. It was chilly but nice. The moon shone bright, surrounded by a blanket of tiny stars. Jamie thought he would have loved standing there admiring such a grand view, had he not been thoroughly soaked in misery. As things stood at the moment, he could not bear the sensation of being so small and insignificant in front of the endless sky. He turned and headed to the stables.

He stammered through the darkness, feeling his way to the switch panel. With his fingers, he found the familiar switches and flipped on only a few of them.

A couple of fluorescent lights flickered on in the alley between the boxes, casting a dim light around.

Jamie heard the scraping of hooves on the ground, the shuffling of huge bodies and annoyed huffs. "Sorry guys..."

He headed toward Acorn's box, his slippers shuffling on the cement pavement. He didn't know why he was going to him. He felt he was walking on autopilot, almost in a trance. He hoped whatever was guiding him was right and he would find what he was looking for.

He unlocked the box and opened the door.

Still lying on the ground, Acorn blinked, his eyes stuck

together with sleep. He glanced up, alert, but as soon as he recognized Jamie, he relaxed and didn't stand up.

Jamie loved that. He loved that Acorn trusted him enough not to jump up when he saw him. Horses were very wary animals and they normally felt too vulnerable on the ground, so they didn't let anybody approach while they were lying down. That was why most people thought they slept standing.

"Hey," Jamie said in a hush. "I'm coming in, all right?"

Acorn studied him, but didn't move.

Jamie drew the door shut and stepped in. As soon as his feet touched the bedding, he felt the wood shavings sneak into his slippers. They crinkled and rolled under his weight, turning into mush. He hated the feeling of wood shavings between his toes, but it was a price he was willing to pay to lie next to his friend.

He kneeled down. "Hey sleepyhead," he said, scratching his neck.

Acorn closed his eyes blissfully.

Jamie felt his skin hot to the touch—he was baking slowly in his sleep. The warmth emanating from him was almost a solid glow all around his body.

"Scooch over," he whispered. He pushed and twisted like a cat trying to find the perfect position. Finally, he propped himself against Acorn's shoulder, drew up his knees and crossed his arms to keep as warm as possible.

Acorn let out a deep sigh of relief.

Jamie enjoyed the warmth of Acorn's body against his back. The big muscles of his shoulders felt couch-like and comfortable—it was like leaning against a heated sofa, a living heated sofa that heaved with every breath.

He tried to relax, but felt too detached from Acorn. He wanted to look at him. Instead, he was staring at the bare door of the box. Within minutes, he sensed all the bad thoughts rushing back at him.

He groaned and turned on his side. He shifted down Acorn's flank a little bit so that he could feel his chest against his ribs. He stuck his hands between his legs and leaned his head against Acorn's shoulder. Acorn's short hair brushed against his cheek, smooth and silky. The warmth of his skin flooded Jamie and traveled down his body as if he had plugged himself into him.

Jamie sighed and looked up at Acorn's face. He watched his huge left eye, round and wet, struggle to stay open, then shut tight into a quick sleep, then open again, cloudy and out of focus. His lower lip hung limp as his long whiskers furrowed the bedding below, picking up wood flakes in their trail. He looked like he was making a mighty effort to stay awake, as if it were his duty to keep him company.

In the silence of the stables, Jamie put his ear against Acorn's side. His massive heart beat at a steady, slow pace, echoing like a drum in the hull of his chest. As he listened, Jamie became aware of the vibration traveling through his own ribs. He started feeling Acorn's heart beating inside him. Slowly, their pulse synced up. Jamie felt the tension abandon his muscles, replaced by the rhythm of Acorn's breathing. The heaving of his enormous chest rocked him gently, hypnotically. All thoughts seeped away and only the vast, deep beat of Acorn's heart filled his mind. His eyes became heavy. He imagined he was traveling the sea inside the belly of a whale. He could hear the water rush outside along the flank of the fish, while inside the hollow trunk the air thumped against his whole body, making him shake in unison with the gigantic heart of the beast.

Jamie gave a start. He looked around stupidly, trying to understand where he was. Quickly, the image of the whale faded away from his eyes and he regained his bearings. He must have fallen asleep. He felt drowsy, his mouth and eyes stuck with sleep. How long he had slept he could not tell, but, because his muscles hurt, he guessed it had been longer than the blink of an eye he felt had passed. Next to him, Acorn was shuffling. That must be why he woke up, he thought. Acorn probably wanted to lie down properly now.

Jamie thought it was better for him to go back to his own bed. He stood up and patted his clothes. A cloud of wood shavings, hay and horse hair enveloped him. He coughed and waved some of the dust away. His skin was itching all over, but he still felt at peace, pleasantly drowsy. He scratched his arms distractedly and stumbled out of the box.

At the door, he emptied his slippers and patted his clothes again. A gentler rain of hay, horse hair, and wood sprinkled around him.

"Thank you, buddy," he said, yawning. "Good night."

Acorn watched him through bleary eyes.

Jamie chuckled at his stupid expression, knowing that it was probably also stamped on his own face. Dumb and dumber, he thought.

He walked back to his bedroom.

Before getting under the covers, he took off his hoodie. It smelled like hay, wood shavings and Acorn—it felt homey. He wished he could keep it on to help him fall asleep, but he knew he couldn't. He threw it in the laundry basket instead. He changed his pajama pants too and washed his feet.

By the time he had finished cleaning up, he was wide awake.

Hoping to get hold of that blissful peace he had felt, he slid under the covers and put a hand on his chest, trying to feel the beat of his own heart. But it wasn't the same. Anxiety crept back inside him with a trail of fears and anger.

11

CRAZY

The next morning, Jamie woke up grumpy and exhausted. Vague, disturbing dreams had kept him tossing and turning all night.

At breakfast, he nibbled without pleasure at his food.

Maddie watched him in silence.

He thought it was better that way; he didn't want to go over their conversation again.

"So, I've been doing some thinking, honey," she said.

Jamie felt his mouth go dry. He swallowed and braced himself.

"You know that if it were up to me, I'd keep you home, but if you miss almost a month and a half of school—plus the days you already missed in the winter—they'll automatically flunk you. I don't want you to lose a year of school. One way or another, I promise you next year you won't have to stand Ms. Ambrose anymore. You think you can make it?"

He thought about it. "Yeah, I think so." He hadn't even considered staying home as a possibility.

Maddie nodded. "Everything will work out, OK? Don't worry. And don't let her scare you. If anything happens, come and tell me. And don't give her any chances to give you bad grades. Lie low."

"OK."

She stood up. "Come on, I'll drive you to school."

Jamie didn't move. "I'd rather bike there, if you don't mind."

Maddie studied him. "You're sure?"

He nodded. "Yeah, it's a nice day. I'd rather bike." He stood up.

"OK, then." Maddie bent down and kissed his cheek. She gently took hold of his chin and turned him around. "Everything will be all right," she repeated.

Jamie nodded and looked away. He hoped she was right. It was bad enough already as it was. He kissed her good-bye and walked out.

While he was riding to school, he started wondering again whether his classmates had told their moms about what had happened. Holly hadn't and instead she had said he lied. But Sara had, and Dan must have too—their moms said they knew, so...

He cringed at the memory of his mom's exchange with the two women. He wished she had already managed to get Ms. Ambrose fired and he could be somewhere else. It wasn't fair that he had to go to class when his teacher beat him. Yet, there he was.

He locked his bike in the back of the school and walked in. A crowd of students of different ages streamed around him. Some he knew, others were complete strangers to him. He wondered whether they were all going through the same trials he was. He arrived in front of the door of his classroom and stepped inside.

His classmates were scattered at random, gossiping and laughing as usual. Jamie sat down at his desk. How could they be so cheerful?

He scanned the room, looking for Dan, and spotted him near

the window, chatting with George and Debbie, a couple of slightly obnoxious kids in his class, both with dark hair and heavy glasses.

He squinted. He hoped to find a bruise or some visible mark on Dan's forehead, but he had pulled his hair down on his forehead. Jamie wasn't sure, but he thought he could make out a slight bump above Dan's right brow. It was much less than he had expected.

He turned around and glanced at the empty seat next to him —Sara was late. She was usually there before him, so she must not feel well or something today.

As he thought that, Sara stepped in. She walked around him without a word and sat down.

"Hi," he greeted her, a bit troubled by her coldness.

"Hi." Sara forced a smile. "I didn't finish my homework, so..." She pulled out her books and set to work.

"Oh, OK..." Jamie left her alone and examined her face: her cheeks were pale and spotted in sickly green blots; her hair stuck out like when you don't get enough sleep; and her eyes were puffy with the lower lids blotched in black. She really did look under the weather. Yet he still wanted to ask her about Ms. Ambrose—It was important. He tried to think of a way to break the question to her, but by the time he had mustered his courage, Ms. Ambrose walked in.

"Good morning, Ms. Ambrose," he said together with the whole class.

"Good morning," she replied benignly.

It was rare for her to answer back, so Jamie took it as a good sign. Better that way; he didn't want any trouble.

Ms. Ambrose sat down at her desk.

Jamie noticed she seemed very calm and collected.

She drew out her register, class notebook, pen and pencils, and laid everything down in neat order before her. Then she looked up, laced her fingers together and surveyed the class-room. "Someone hasn't been a good child here..."

He felt a plunge in his stomach as the hair on the back of his neck stood up. His mind went suddenly numb.

Ms. Ambrose heaved a weary sigh and took off her glasses. "I know that someone told tales about me. Everything I do, I do it for your own good and it's not right for you to go out and tell your parents what happens between us. You know, nobody likes a snitch." Suddenly, she glanced at Jamie.

He tore his eyes away from her as quickly as possible. She knew! She knew it was him... How could she know? Could she read his mind? The look she had given him... He felt a rush of heat run through his body and the back of his shirt became sticky with sweat. He felt naked, defenseless. What was she going to do to him now? He swayed at the prospect of being slapped like Dan.

"These things should stay between us," Ms. Ambrose continued calmly. "I'm just teaching you how to learn, how to become better children, to make you smarter and better in life. I am your teacher, your friend. It's not right to talk behind a friend's back. You need to learn to be good children or next time I won't be able to be so nice, OK?" She put her glasses back on, opened the textbook in front of her and said, "Now open your books to page fifty-six."

It took Jamie a few seconds to recover. She wasn't going to punish him? Why? What was she doing? He couldn't wrap his head around what was happening. Had she forgiven him? She didn't look angry... She called him a snitch, though. Why did she call him that? He didn't want his classmates to think he was a liar and a backstabber. He wasn't; he had told the truth. Was he really the only one who had talked? His insides squirmed. He couldn't be the only one who had told his mom... Sara had, and Dan too—his mom said she knew, so...

The bell rang.

Jamie gave a start—he had completely lost track of time. He waited for Ms. Ambrose to walk out of the classroom, then turned to Sara. "You told your mom too, right, that Ms. Ambrose hit Dan?"

She blinked and the color suddenly drained from her face. "No," she said in a choked whisper, shaking her head.

Jamie opened his mouth to say something, then closed it. Wait, what? No? His brain stumbled. "You didn't see Ms. Ambrose slap Dan and me!?"

"No."

"But your mom said you told her."

"I didn't say anything. Ms. Ambrose didn't do anything."

"But—"

"I don't want to talk about it!"

Jamie flinched.

Sara snatched her lunch from her backpack and stormed out.

He blushed. He had been sure Sara told her mom. She was sitting next to him—she must have seen. But she just said she didn't. Was it true? Was he crazy, then? Or was she lying? But why would she lie to him? He frowned and turned around to face Debbie and George, who sat right behind him. "You saw what happened, right?"

They looked at each other, then shook their heads nervously.

Jamie felt a strange veil wrap around him as if he had entered an alternate reality. What was going on? He watched stupidly as Debbie and George sneaked out of their seats and hurried out of the room like two rats jumping off a sinking ship.

Something was wrong. He pulled himself up. This wasn't happening, he thought. They had all seen it. They couldn't say it did not happen.

In a daze, he walked out and approached the first group of

his classmates he spotted. It was Holly and Francesca, sitting on the rock sculpture in the middle of the garden, eating their lunch and chatting.

"You saw Ms. Ambrose slap Dan yesterday, right?"

The girls turned.

"No," Francesca replied bluntly and turned around.

No? Really? They were sitting in the first row—everything happened right behind them. Jamie frowned and turned to Holly, who was still looking at him. "You neither?"

Holly hesitated, but before she could say anything, Francesca pulled her around. "No, she didn't. Now scram, we're trying to eat our lunch!"

Jamie spun around as if he had been slapped. Was he dreaming? Why was everyone denying Dan had been hit? Did he imagine it? Did he saw it wrong? He searched his memory. Clear as a cut still bleeding, the image of Dan's head bouncing against his desk stood out before his eyes. No, it happened. Then why were all of his classmates behaving as if it never did? Was it because of Ms. Ambrose? Were they afraid of her?

He felt like he had been cast off from a mountain, falling endlessly down through the air with nothing to cling to. He spotted Alex under a tree nearby, eating his lunch and talking to Daniel Maltby, another classmate of his. He ran up to them.

"Hey!"

Alex and Daniel nodded to him.

"You saw Ms. Ambrose slap me and Dan, right?"

"Why do you want to know?" Alex asked suspiciously.

"Ehm…" he fumbled. He didn't expect that question. "I told my mom. I just wanted to know if you did too. My mom said that if we all get together, we can get her fired."

"Didn't you hear what Ms. Ambrose said? I didn't see anything."

Jamie blinked and turned to Daniel. He shot him a look and shook his head.

Again, he felt he had hit a brick wall. Anger and desperation started mounting up inside him. What was going on? He did a one-eighty and veered aimlessly back toward school. He spotted Luka. He wouldn't care, he thought. He's not scared of anybody. He headed toward him.

As soon as Luka saw him approach, he picked up a handful of pebbles and flung them at him.

Jamie dodged the pelting rain and changed course. He felt like a ship that had gone adrift. He spotted Dan eating his lunch alone, sitting in the grass on the slope at the edge of the school fence. OK, he thought, everybody else could say whatever they wanted, but Dan would back him up. He had helped him. He got kicked because he was trying to protect him.

Dan heard his steps approaching and glanced up.

"Hi!"

Dan blushed and looked away. "Hi..." he mumbled reluctantly.

"So..." Jamie said, but he felt the words die in his throat. "You... you told your mom Ms. Ambrose hit you yesterday, right?"

Dan flinched. "Nobody hit me!"

Anger flared up inside Jamie like a wildfire—this was too much! "What do you mean nobody hit you!? She slapped you so hard, your head bounced against the desk!"

"You're crazy!" Dan blurted, springing to his feet.

"What are you talking about!? She HIT you!" He wanted to grab him, shake him until he admitted Ms. Ambrose had hurt him, punch him until he told the truth. He started toward him.

Dan winced and bolted toward the entrance.

Jamie spun around and froze—people all around the garden were staring at him. He retreated, clenching his fists, his whole body shaking with anger and frustration. What was going on? He felt as if he was somewhere else, yet at the same time there, as if he had entered a parallel reality, a twilight zone. What was happening was simply impossible. Is this how mad people felt? Everybody was saying that nothing happened, that he had dreamed of Ms. Ambrose slapping Dan. Why were they doing this to him? Were they lying? All of them? How could so many people lie all at once? Was he going mad? And Dan, how could he lie? The image of Dan's head smashing against his desk flashed in front of his eyes again, but this time it lingered and became fuzzier. Had he really seen it? Was he sure? He studied his memory again. Did he misunderstand? Maybe Dan's forehead didn't bounce against the desk... maybe he just ducked... maybe he ducked and hit his head against the desk by mistake...

As he thought that, Jamie heard in his mind the slap of Ms. Ambrose's hand against Dan's head, then the smacking sound of his forehead on the flat surface of the desk. No, he hadn't imagined it. He hadn't. He was sure, yet the sense of unreality still stuck to him.

They were all lying then...

How could it be? Jamie still couldn't come to grips with it. Telling the truth was the right thing to do, so why were they lying?

He felt like choking, like drowning. He gasped for air and blinked around. He saw his classmates, but they looked distant, two dimensional, as if they were tokens for something else he could not recognize anymore. He felt a sudden urge to run home, to hide, to sleep. But he couldn't; he knew he couldn't. He turned around and headed toward his classroom. Behind him, somebody coughed and slurred, "Snitch!"

Jamie stopped in his tracks and wheeled around. Nobody was looking at him anymore. They were all turned away, chatting among themselves. Had he imagined it? Before he could figure it out, the bell rang. Slowly, almost in a trance, he turned around and walked back to his classroom.

He sat down and stared without seeing at the blackboard. It was only when he heard the groans of disapproval coming from his classmates that his eyes focused on the white lines drawn in chalk on the blackboard. A sign in capital letters read: ESSAY TOPICS.

He blinked. Ms. Ambrose wanted him to write an essay after all that had happened? His brain floundered at the mere prospect of having to output something. Yet, he had no choice unless he wanted to get a bad grade. His father would certainly understand, he thought sarcastically. No, he did not want a bad grade. He craned forward and read the first topic:

Take these lines from a well-known novel and continue them however you want: She had found a jewel down inside herself and she wanted to walk where people could see her and gleam it around...

Good for whoever 'she' was, Jamie thought. He had not. He didn't want to write about something that he already felt envious about. He scanned down to the second topic:

Best friends are special people in our lives. Before you begin writing, think about your best friend and the reasons why he/she is your best friend. Now explain to the reader why this person is your best friend.

Jamie frowned and glanced at his classmates. Friends... Was there really anybody here who he could call his best friend? After what they had done? He peeked at his side. Sara Winters? He didn't think so. She had lied to him and now she wasn't even talking to him anymore. He turned. Holly? Maybe Holly when they were little, but not now. She didn't care anymore. She was too busy with Francesca. Dan? Jamie felt his stomach squirm tight. Dan had called him crazy; he had lied; he had shunned him even after he had helped him. No, Dan wasn't his friend. And the rest? Snitch! the slur echoed in his mind.

He turned around and glared at the blackboard. They didn't deserve to be called friends! Only Acorn did. But he was a horse, and he knew too well what people thought about that. He shrugged—they were wrong.

He threw another glance around. The room was full of people, but he felt alone, completely alone. Friends... Why couldn't they go back to the time when they all still played together? Why had things become so awful? If only he could get out of school and never come back. Acorn would be happy.

Suddenly he imagined Acorn, miles away, turning his dark, wet eyes toward him and pricking up his ears. A ray of warmth cracked through the shell of his despair. He was never alone. Never. Acorn was always there with him. A weak smile wrinkled his lips. He sighed and started writing.

12

WANDERING

J amie stared into space, lost in thought.

Acorn charged. He skidded to a halt a few feet from him and reared up.

Jamie didn't flinch.

Acorn snorted. He bolted forward and reared up again.

Clumps of sand flew in the air and splattered against Jamie's chest. The huge mass of Acorn's body rose ominously over him. Jamie gave a start, scooped up a handful of sand and hurled it at Acorn. He jolted around and kicked back.

Jamie watched as one of his hooves whipped the air a couple of feet from his head. "Hey!" he shouted angrily.

Acorn broke into a gallop, kicking and neighing.

Jamie knew that he just wanted to play, but that was too close a shave. Crazy horse... He really didn't know when a joke was going too far. He better teach Acorn some restraint, or one of these days he was going to kick his head in. After all, he was a thousand-pound animal, not a little dog. A kick of his would break his bones as if they were toothpicks.

Acorn stopped in the center of the school, behind one of the three tall cement pillars that housed the spotlights for the evening riding lessons. He pretended the object could hide him and glanced back expectantly.

Jamie sighed—Acorn wanted to play hide-and-seek. He was so weird when he did that. Jamie had seen dogs behave in that peculiar way—hiding behind a blade of grass or a sprig and pretending their master couldn't see them—but he had never seen a horse other than Acorn do that. All right... He dragged his feet forward, searching around, feigning he hadn't spotted him.

Acorn in turn remained perfectly still, his eyes the only thing moving in his body.

Jamie sidled closer to the cement pillar, looking away, then he spun around and clapped his hands loudly.

Acorn jerked back and galloped away, flaring his nostrils in a satisfied rush of adrenaline.

Jamie smiled weakly at his contentment and waited for him to place himself behind another one of the pillars. He felt the energy drain away from his limbs at the prospect of some more silly play—he was just not in the mood. He turned around and spotted his mom waving at him as she stepped into the school. He walked eagerly toward her—he knew Acorn would leave him alone for a little bit if he saw he was busy with someone else.

"Hi, kitten!" She gave him a peck on the cheek.

"Hi, Mom."

"Was your snack all right?"

He nodded and looked away. She had left some chicken stew on the stove for him, but when he had come back from school, he had been so upset that he didn't even feel like warming it up. He had simply taken the Pyrex bowl, laid it on the table, and sunken the fork in. His intention had been to take a couple of bites, but in less than ten minutes he had swallowed all the chicken almost without chewing, without even tasting it. He had stuffed himself like that in order to bury the shame and anger that seared his stomach, but he had ended up only feeling worse. An hour later, the inordinate amount of food he had piled up inside him still pressed as if it wanted to tear his guts apart. At this point, he was sure it would take him all day to digest what felt like a stone in his belly.

Maddie looked at his sullen expression and darkened. "Did she do anything today?"

Jamie looked up. "No, but she knew I had talked to you. She said she's our friend and I snitched on her."

Maddie narrowed her eyes. "Did she say that?"

Jamie hesitated. "Well… She said these things should stay between us and that she was our teacher and friend. She said nobody likes a snitch. She was talking to everybody, but she gave me this look. I think she knows. How does she know?"

Maddie snorted. "Dear Mrs. Winters must have tipped off her parish buddy."

Right, Jamie thought, of course… Mrs. Winters and Ms. Ambrose were friends—Mrs. Winters had said that. Why didn't he think of that? Why did he think instead that Ms. Ambrose had some kind of power, that she could read his mind or something? He felt a bit relieved to know she was only human, yet he was still frustrated at himself for being so stupid.

"What's wrong?"

Jamie looked away. "My classmates said it didn't happen."

Maddie frowned.

"They said they didn't see anything. Sara said she didn't say anything to her mom, and Dan…" Jamie shook his head in disbelief. "He said Ms. Ambrose didn't hit him. How…?" He shook his head again, struggling with the concept. "How can he say that? I saw it."

"They are lying, Jamie. I'm not surprised."

She wasn't? He was. He didn't expect that. He never expected it. He still couldn't believe it.

"This is enough," she groaned. "I and Ms. Ambrose are going to have a nice little chat face to face!"

Jamie winced. "No, no, it's all right." He didn't want any more trouble. He was scared about what his classmates would do to him if he insisted. They were even worse than Ms. Ambrose.

"No, it's not all right, Jamie," Maddie said, looking him in the eyes. "That—" She bit her lip, holding in a curse. "It did happen," she stroked his hair, "and she's not your friend. I believe you."

He shrugged. It gave him some relief to know that his mom believed him, but it didn't matter that much. Nobody else did. They had told him he was crazy, that he dreamt up things, that he was a liar, a backstabber, a snitch. They said that things that happened didn't. He felt again a wave of unreality hurtle toward him and drown him. It was as if a pack of stray dogs had singled him out and was circling around, ready to tear him to pieces. He had seen dogs do that. Somehow, they smelled the other animal was sick or weak and they attacked to finish it. It was an instinct to destroy that he couldn't understand. He didn't feel weak or sick, though, so why were his classmates attacking him? He hadn't done anything wrong. He only told the truth. They should have done the same, so why were they instead hurting him?

Maddie glanced up and shook her head. "You better take him for a ride before he tears down the whole school."

Jamie turned around. Acorn beamed at him in triumph with a rail in his mouth. He must have picked it up off of one of the obstacles and was now ready to parade it around. With the skin of his upper lip stretched back and his thumb-sized teeth exposed, he looked insane. Probably he was. What else can a horse that did stuff like that be?

At such a sight, Jamie would have usually laughed, but his face felt like frozen lead today. He shook his head weakly—Mom was right, there was no way Acorn would leave him alone unless he helped him let off some steam. Apparently, the trip to the river the day before had charged him up, instead of tiring him.

"I'll see you later, OK?" Maddie said and kissed him good-bye. "You two be careful!"

He nodded and looked back at Acorn, who was trotting around with the rail in his mouth and his tail up, exceedingly proud of his deed. Maybe it would do him good to have to deal with him, he thought. It would take his mind away from his troubles. He didn't feel like going on one of their little trips, though. It might be the first time he felt that way. "C'mon, loony," he called, "let's go!"

He saddled and bridled Acorn listlessly. It took him way longer than it should have to get ready, but finally, he mounted and they were off. He decided to head toward the lake on the other side of the hill that rose in front of the house. It was a nice day, so there was probably going to be a great view. He cut through the woods.

He led Acorn off the track and made him climb the steep hill straight up. That would cut his breath, he thought, and hopefully some of his steam too.

Acorn puffed uphill like a train. After a couple of minutes, he started sweating, but he didn't give any signs of wanting to slow down. Instead, he seemed to enjoy the effort.

Better that way, Jamie thought. At least one of them was having a good time. He bent forward and held tight to Acorn's mane, steadying himself.

When they arrived at the top of the hill, Acorn was finally panting—his nostrils heaving in huge gasps of air. He sighed with relief as they took a flat track and slowed down.

Jamie tried to lose himself in the rhythm of his body, but he couldn't. He felt detached, just a guest on the back of this amazing animal. He couldn't be one with him today. A stinging sadness laid over his already crushing despair. He just wished he could get hit out cold by a low branch on the track and lose his memory. That way, maybe he'd wake up feeling himself again.

As the minutes passed, Acorn tensed up, his ears twitching right and left, his gait becoming jagged.

Jamie noticed it and knew it was his own fault. He couldn't let go, he couldn't forget what his classmates had done to him. And the problem wasn't just today... He had to see them tomorrow too, and the day after tomorrow, and the day after that. His stomach sank at the prospect of being around them any more time. He didn't want to inhabit the same world as these people who could deny reality, who could deny truth. No, he didn't want to, but what other choice did he have? He wished he could sneak through a wrinkle in reality and pop out in a different world where people didn't lie.

He felt trapped—trapped in his own body, trapped in this town, trapped in his life as terrible things were closing in on him. He had never felt this way before. Nothing had ever been easy—he was poor—but he had never felt trapped. He had always been able to make the best out of things. Now he felt he may not have the strength or the power or the will to do it. How could he change the mind of all the people around him?

His head started spinning—he couldn't. If it had depended on him, he could have done something, but this had nothing to do with him. Or maybe it had. Maybe it had everything to do with him... He didn't like that thought. There wasn't anything wrong with him. He just told the truth!

The memory of that wonderful school trip to his house a few years ago flooded his mind. The faces of his classmates smiling at him with admiration swam in front of his eyes. Why had things changed so much? Was it his fault? What had he done to deserve this? He wanted that happiness back. He wanted his friends back!

He grunted and tried to shake the awful angst that was weighing him down. He spurred Acorn to a trot. He needed to stop thinking. He urged Acorn to a gallop in the narrow track. Focus! he ordered himself. Focus on the track, on the stones, on the rhythm of Acorn's steps, on the branches coming at you!

It didn't work. After being lashed in the face a couple of times, he slowed back down to a walk. His eyes streaming, he held his hands over his face, blinking. At least, that pain was sharp enough to clear everything else away from his mind for a minute or two.

When they finally arrived at the lake, the view was beautiful: the water shimmered in the afternoon sun while a light breeze brushed the reeds and woods nearby. Ducks and swans glided on the green surface of the water, while some red-necked grebes dived and reemerged around them. Jamie's brain registered the objective beauty of the landscape, but no emotion followed that realization.

An hour and a half later, they were back at the farmstead. Jamie glanced at his watch and realized that three hours had passed since they had gone out, but to him it felt as if he had only left the stables a few minutes ago—time didn't seem to flow as usual anymore.

He unsaddled Acorn and let him free in the paddock.

Sweaty and satisfied, he started smelling around like a hound. As soon as he found the best dusty patch of earth, he kneeled down on his side and rolled around vigorously from side to side, raising a billowing cloud of dirt.

Jamie watched him enjoy his dust bath with perfect bliss and found himself unable to share his satisfaction. He felt as if they had cleaved his soul in two, as if he had been wrenched away from himself and didn't know the way back anymore. Lost, he turned around and headed home.

As he got into the kitchen, he grabbed some cocoa powder,

milk and potato starch to make hot chocolate. He decided maybe that would do him some good. Maybe the warmth, sweetness and richness of the chocolate could restore some feeling inside him.

As he was whisking the chocolate powder into the warm milk, he heard the sound of the gate being pulled open and the car driving through. Mom had returned. He hoped she had good news. He heard her walk through the door and turned around— she looked livid. Oh, no, he thought, bracing himself.

"What are you making?"

"Hot chocolate."

"Gimme, I'll do it." She nudged him away and slipped the spoon out of his hand. "Sit down."

Jamie let her take charge. He didn't even have the strength to feel dread anymore. He knew something bad was coming, but he could only sit there, waiting for it to strike him.

For a few minutes, the only sound in the kitchen was the clicking and rasping of the whisk against the metal lid of the milk pan. Then, the warm aroma of cocoa finally filled the room.

Maddie turned off the heat, poured the hot chocolate in Jamie's favorite mug and sat down with him.

"Thank you." He stared at the hot beverage as if he didn't know what to do with it. He wasn't sure why, but he didn't feel like drinking it in front of his mom. He wanted to be alone.

"So, I went to your school," Maddie said. "I had already made an appointment with the principal, but since I had to wait, I went directly to your teacher."

Jamie's fingers tightened around the mug. Here we go again, he thought, bracing himself. He just wanted to shut his ears, but knew it was useless: his mom was going to tell him everything no matter what. Why did she have to make him go through this? A vague hope that she might have something nice to say flickered inside him, but it died almost instantly. He knew from her expression that only hurt was coming.

"I went there and the door was open," Maddie continued, "I stepped in—the other moms were right outside, waiting for their turn. I walked up to Ms. Ambrose and told her: Listen, I'm here to inquire about your justification for what you've done to my son. And about what you're doing to the other children.

"She stiffened and replied: Why, what are you talking about?

"I'm talking about the fact that you're beating your pupils, I said.

"What? That's absolutely not true!"

She too said that nothing had happened, Jamie thought angrily. Why did they all keep on doing this?

"Since that was her reply, I said: Listen, don't even try and play me, because I'm already furious enough. Save yourself the time and don't tell me it's not true, because I know it is.

"Ms. Ambrose crossed her arms and looked down at me. She probably thought she could handle me. I don't know what you're talking about, she repeated.

"I'm talking about you hitting my son and smashing another one of his classmate's head against his own desk, I said.

"Oh, this is it? Your son is blowing things out of proportion. I just slapped him lightly on the back of his head because he was being rude. He just needed corrective punishment and that's what I did. It's normal."

I wasn't being rude, Jamie thought furiously. I was trying to help Dan!

"Normal for her maybe," Maddie sneered. "No, I told her, if my son needs punishment, I'll administer it, not you. These methods don't suit me and don't you ever think you can take the liberty, even if the law permitted it—and it doesn't—to use violence against my son.

"She waved my comment aside and said: You are just going

into hysterics now. Kids lie. They blow things out of proportion all the time."

The others lie for sure, Jamie thought bitterly, but I don't!

"Absolutely not, I told her. My son came home completely shocked. Plus, now I understand. Often, in the morning, Jamie drinks his milk and vomits. That is a clear sign of stress—I asked my doctor. That means you put him under such pressure that he couldn't even keep his food down. What you're doing is disgusting! You're using our kids for personal gain to make it look like you're the best teacher around.

"As an answer, she stiffened and said: I am the best teacher around!

"No, you are an animal, I replied. How dare you take it out on children!"

Wow, Jamie thought. Did Mom actually call her that? Wow.

Maddie smiled icily. "Poor Ms. Ambrose took offense and puffed up like a turkey, trying to intimidate me. What do you know!? she said. You think you can come here with these accusations and question my educational methods!?

"Don't even try to take me for a fool, I said immediately. I can and I do question them indeed! You keep your hands off my son. And not only that, you'll also not lay a hand on any of the other kids, because I do not tolerate violence in the classroom. There are other methods that you should know how to use.

"I do whatever I want! she exploded.

"Oh, no, no, no, you don't. Are we sure it's the kids that need some corrective action and not you instead that need some help? There's the therapist for that, you know.

"How dare you speak to me like that! Ms. Ambrose shouted at me, livid with anger, I have a reputation. I do whatever I want!"

Jamie held his breath. He knew too well how dangerous it was to make his teacher mad.

"Once again, no, you don't! I said. I had been polite and kept my voice down till then, but since she raised hers, I let her have it. I yelled out clear and loud so that all of the other mothers outside could hear me: You really think you can go around and hit my son and all of his classmates every day!? And slam their heads against their own desks!? And kick them!? And threaten them that if they talk, you won't give them good grades anymore!? And if they tell their moms, that they're snitches!? And that what happens in the classroom stays in the classroom!? We're not in the Dark Ages, do you hear me!? You can't beat and brainwash children anymore and come to me saying it's an educational method. If you can't teach, change careers dear, because you're not good at this!

"Ms. Ambrose turned purple and struggled to reply, but nothing came out of her mouth, so I went on: My son has only another month and a half left. I don't want to take him out of school right now, because you might very well flunk him out of spite, but I warn you, if he comes home and tells me that you did so much as touch him or any other of the children, or yell at them, or use one of your 'methods', watch out, because I'll go to social services and the police right away. I was kind enough not to go already. I hope you will be reasonable."

Could she really do that? Jamie wondered. Why hadn't she done it already then?

"At that Ms. Ambrose magically calmed down," Maddie said sarcastically. "OK, OK, sure, she said. Don't take it like that. There is no reason to get so upset. It wasn't that bad. It was just a slap, but whatever you say. Really, there is no need to make such a fuss.

"What a tool she is!" Maddie growled. "The other moms had listened and watched the whole conversation, but they didn't say a word and parted when I came out. As I was walking toward the exit though, when Emily's mom came up to me.

"Hi, excuse me, she said. I heard you; I was just outside. I wanted to tell you that you're right. There had been some gossip about Ms. Ambrose, but my daughter never told me anything, so I thought it was just people being mean and such, but obviously it's not the case. I totally agree with you, so if you want to do something together—

"Thank you, but just the two of us won't make any difference, I said, and left."

Jamie frowned. Why did she blow her off? Emily's mom wanted to help. Perhaps the other moms would have joined in too if she had let Emily's mom in. Why did she say no? The first person who finally wanted to be on their side and she blew her off.

"Since I didn't obtain anything from the teacher," Maddie continued, "I went to my appointment with the principal."

Jamie looked away, worn out. Mom told off Ms. Ambrose, but that was it. She didn't really manage to do anything or to scare her, so why was she telling him? He didn't want to listen anymore.

"I went in. We greeted and Mr. Culvert offered me a chair.

"How can I help you today, Mrs. Blackshear? he asked with fake politeness."

He too, Jamie thought, sensing the angry sarcasm in his mom's voice. Are they really all like that?

Maddie sighed. "I started all over again and said: Well, I have come to let you know that Ms. Ambrose beats her pupils. My son was just slapped and kicked the other day while a classmate of his got his head smashed against his own desk. I asked my son why he never told me and he said because Ms. Ambrose told them that what happens in class is something 'between them' and it must stay so. She also intimated that if the kids told their moms, then she wouldn't give them good grades anymore.

"Mr. Culvert smiled condescendingly at me, then said: Ms.

Ambrose is our best teacher and the best in the district. I'm a little bit tired of overapprehensive mothers who come and complain their kids are not treated well enough. They're never treated well enough. Ms. Ambrose is an excellent teacher and the pillar of our school.

"I seriously wanted to set fire to him, but I stayed calm," Maddie said through clenched teeth.

Jamie instead felt the urge to run away, far, far away from these awful people.

"She may even be considered the best teacher in the district, I said. I don't doubt it. But, in my opinion, she's the worst. It's no method to beat a child to make him perform better. And whatever others think, I don't condone it. So, I'm here to inquire about your intentions, because—otherwise—I'll take different measures.

"Oh, come on, Mrs. Blackshear, please, Mr. Culvert told me. After all, a flick on the head that makes hair fly never hurt anybody. On the contrary, it's a very effective educational method that's been used for ages."

Jamie winced. Was it really? For sure, they all seemed awfully OK with it, parents, teachers and the principal too. Only he and his mom had spoken out against it. Were they wrong?

Maddie sneered. "Oh, really? I said. You're talking to somebody that went through the old school. They even made us kneel with our hands under our knees and whipped us with the stick. It's a shameful, stupid thing. If a teacher doesn't have the ability to convince children and make them think, she should change jobs. It's no excuse that it is difficult to deal with a class of thirty kids."

Jamie looked up. He had never known Mom had gone through that. It must have been awful.

"Mr. Culvert didn't reply and glowered at me, so I went on: Anyway, I just learned something today. If you say that, educationally speaking, a flick on the head that makes hair fly is so effective, then wait here a second while I call my husband on the phone, so he can come here and slap you in the face. Then we'll see if you still think the same!

"Mr. Culvert flinched at that. Ha!"

Jamie grinned. Take that!

"Aaaah, you see, I said. You talk the talk and it's all good for you when other people get hit, but you don't like that to happen to you, do you?

"He didn't answer, but shot me a nasty look.

"Right, I went on. Nobody likes it. At this point I just want to transfer my son to another class—

"I won't allow that, he cut in immediately. There is no reason to do it."

Jamie's grin collapsed.

"I paused to make sure he understood clearly what I was about to say: Look, I'm not asking for your permission. I'm doing all the required steps to obtain it. You just better hope that I don't have to go to the police, because I won't stop then.

"Despite the threat, he didn't ruffle a feather and instead sneered at me, then said formally: You can submit an application in writing to my attention if you wish, but I am telling you, nothing will happen. Your son is not transferring to another class, Mrs. Blackshear.

"Very well then, I replied, standing up. I see you sit on a chair you don't deserve. Good-bye, Mr. Culvert. And I left."

Jamie blinked and looked away. So that hadn't worked either. He really hoped that was all, because he didn't know if he could take any more bad news.

"This is a rotten town," Maddie grumbled.

Yeah, Jamie thought, it is.

"Anyway, don't worry. I'll transfer you to another school. Don't worry, OK?"

Jamie felt her hand brushing his hair and frowned. He didn't think transferring was going to make a difference at this point, but so be it. Plus, she had been repeating not to worry way too many times by now. He was starting to get anxious every time she said it. And why on Earth did she kept on telling him these stories if she wanted him not to worry? He didn't want to hear about how nasty people were—he already knew too well. Instead, he wanted to get away from them. Transferring was fine. Anything to steer clear of them.

"There is a trick we can use," Maddie said, lost in thought.

Jamie wondered what she meant, but he didn't feel like asking. He wanted the conversation to be over.

Maddie stood up and went to wash the dishes.

Jamie remained at the table, frozen. He felt as if he were sinking through the chair. He wished he could disappear.

13

THE ESSAY

"Good morning, Ms. Ambrose," Jamie said together with his classmates.

She didn't answer and instead sat down, pulled the stack of essays from her leather bag and slapped it on the desk.

That was quick, Jamie thought—it usually took her almost a week to correct their essays. He sighed. So, today he was going to get a grade... He really hoped it was a decent one because he didn't want to deal with any more negative stuff. My best friend, he recited in his head. A flood of memories filled him as he remembered all the good times he had spent with Acorn. Too many to fit in the essay. He had done his best to pick the right ones that would show his character and give reasons why he was such an amazing friend. The image of Acorn trotting around with the rail in his mouth, beaming at him with crazed eyes, flashed in his mind.

Jamie frowned, struck by an epiphany. He suddenly wondered if all the scenes Acorn had put up the day before were actually attempts to get him to feel better, to entertain him and tell him to get out of his funk. He had no way of knowing if that was true, but he had a hunch Acorn had really tried to cheer him up.

Despite all the gloom, the absurdity of what had happened with his classmates and the angst he felt, Jamie couldn't suppress a smile. He had done the right thing in writing about Acorn—he really was his best friend. He wished he could bring the essay home right away and show it to him. If he could have understood, Jamie was sure Acorn would have been really proud of being the absolute and sole star of his paper.

Ms. Ambrose turned to the class and announced, "We're going to read your essays aloud today."

Jamie's smile collapsed like a house of cards. The thought hadn't even occurred to him. Why didn't he think of that? He didn't want to read his paper in front of the class. He didn't want his classmates to know that he preferred Acorn to them. What would they think? Stupid, stupid, stupid! Why did he always do things without thinking? It was no excuse they almost never read their essays in class. But why did it have to be now of all times?

Ms. Ambrose opened the register and called, "Andrei, George."

Behind Jamie, George stood up and strode to the desk. He started reading.

Jamie felt like a cow waiting in line at the slaughterhouse. He tried to listen to what his classmates had written, but he couldn't focus. He stared at Ms. Ambrose's desk as if it were the gallows, his sense of dread mounting as his classmates filed in front of him.

"Andrews, Brittany."

"Barnaby, Debbie."

"Blackshear, Jamie."

He stood up and strode to the desk—better get it over with quickly. He took the essay from Ms. Ambrose and faced the classroom. For a split second, he thought that maybe this was actually a good thing. Perhaps this was his chance to get his friends back. Maybe his classmates wouldn't laugh when they listened to him talk about Acorn; they would instead remember the good times of that day during the school trip, and they would want to come back. He really hoped they didn't laugh. He shifted his weight uncomfortably and felt his feet, sweaty and cold, writhing like worms in his shoes.

Ms. Ambrose laced her fingers together, waiting.

Jamie gathered himself and started, "My best friend is not the ordinary type. He is bay, five-five at his withers, and his name is Acorn. Let me tell you something: if you've never caressed the soft spot on his nose, you're missing something in your life. It's like velvet." He looked up for a second—everybody was listening.

"Kiss it, pet it, or just rub it against your cheek, and you're sure going to have a good day. Acorn was born from my dad's mare Carlie and a stallion we call Sand. I actually not only am Acorn's best friend, but also his godfather, because I was the only one present when Carlie delivered him, and I was there to applaud him when he walked for the first time.

"A best friend is somebody you can count on. Somebody that loves you and is always there for you. Acorn is just like that. He's always there when I'm sad, and we play together, and when it's warm outside we swim in the river. I couldn't ask for a better friend in the whole world even if I tried."

Jamie caught his breath and glanced up. His classmates were still listening, although some of them were whispering to each other. They weren't sniggering or anything like that though. Thank goodness. He lowered his eyes and started reading again.

"Sometimes, I wish we could talk, so that we could share more things. I don't know if that really is the right thing, though, because a friendship that doesn't need words is something very special. Being friends with someone of another species is magical and I'm not sure things could be better if Acorn could speak.

"Acorn is also very funny and makes me laugh a lot. He loves candy and whenever I let him try a new flavor, his eyes become huge and round. He makes this surprised face and you can almost see fireworks going off in his brain—"

"That's enough," cut in Ms. Ambrose as she pulled the essay out of his hands.

Jamie was taken aback. Was it so bad that she had to stop him midway through? He thought he had done a good job. He was about to get to the good stuff. He glanced nervously at his classmates. They were all craning their necks, whispering to each other. At least they hadn't laughed. He didn't want a bad grade, though. He turned back just in time to see Ms. Ambrose writing a big red C on the front page of the essay. He gaped. "C!?"

"You didn't do the assignment, Jamie."

"What? Acorn is my best friend!"

"A horse is your best friend? I think your mother keeps you locked up in your farm too much!"

The classroom suddenly exploded with laughter.

Jamie whipped around, stunned. There was something horrible in his classmates' glee, something violent. He searched for a face that wasn't contorted in that contemptuous snigger, but even Holly was laughing. Only Sara wasn't mocking him, but she was giving him a look so full of pity, it made him sick. It looked as if she thought he was stupid or something. "Stop it!" he shouted.

His classmates roared even louder.

Their laughter stung. Jamie glared at them, shaking with anger, tears welling up in the back of his throat. Why did he always have to feel like crying when all he wanted was to lash out? He swallowed and turned back. Ms. Ambrose was chuckling too. Jamie stood nailed to the spot. How could she do that? How could she laugh in his face? She was his teacher.

"Well, you see it for yourself, dear. You should be friends with your classmates, not with an animal."

Jamie flushed.

She gave him back his essay and spoke slowly as if his IQ had suddenly dropped twenty points. "It is very cute of you, but a pet is not a person, Jamie. They don't have a personality."

What!? What was she talking about? Had she ever been around an animal? That was completely wrong! How could she give him a bad grade if she didn't know what she was talking about? "Have you ever had a pet?"

Ms. Ambrose's gaze hardened; she raised her brow. "No, and I don't need to."

Ignorant, Jamie growled in his head. And presumptuous! He knew better than her, but she wouldn't even listen to him. How could she be a teacher!?

Ms. Ambrose threw a fleeting glance back at the essay and a smile resurfaced on her lips. "Next time, I want you to write something real, all right?" she said with unfiltered condescension.

Jamie wanted to punch her in the face. He wanted to shout at her and kick her. The blood drained from his face as he repressed his rage. Stiffly, he walked back to his desk and sat down, his ears buzzing. As soon as it came, the laughter went away. His classmates were now ignoring him. The silence stunned Jamie. For a second, he wondered whether he had imagined it all. He didn't care that Ms. Ambrose was being stupid with him, but his classmates had laughed. Their roaring cackle still resounded in his head.

Shame filled him like a sinking ship. He felt a dull darkness seep inside him through his skin, through his eyes. Everything slowed down around him, went muffled and out of focus. Time flowed thick like molasses, then thankfully the bell rang.

The classroom quickly emptied. He stayed behind.

Sara fumbled with her lunch for an unnecessarily long time, then squeezed out behind him. She made a couple of steps toward the door, then suddenly spun around. "Jamie..."

He glanced up.

"I... I like horses too!"

Jamie frowned. "OK..." And so what?

She opened her mouth to say something, then she changed her mind, blushed and sneaked away.

Jamie glared at her as she disappeared through the door. Was she stupid? Why the hell did she tell him that? What was the point? She hadn't talked to him at all and then she just stopped to say she liked horses!? He couldn't care less! What kind of a stupid comment was that!?

He gnawed his teeth, his stomach lurching unpleasantly, and struggled to calm down. He dropped the essay in his backpack, hoping that if he didn't see it, he would feel better. He picked up his sandwich and headed doggedly into the hallway. All he wanted was to get to his favorite spot in the garden and eat in peace.

As he walked out of the classroom, he felt the hair on the back of his neck stand up. Something in the air was wrong. He searched around, trying to identify the source of his disquiet, but he couldn't pinpoint anything specific. Kids were all gathered in groups in the hallway, minding their own business, but there was a strange immobility to the scene.

He slowed down as if to muffle his steps and sneak through

the crowd unobserved. He couldn't shake the presentiment that something bad was looming on him. He was halfway through when somebody behind him made a sound like a neigh.

Jamie wheeled around, but immediately realized that was the wrong thing to do. He looked, but couldn't tell who had done it. They got him! Kids were already laughing at his confusion. From the other end of the hallway, somebody else neighed. Jamie spun around despite himself.

Luka sneered from the side wall. "Hello, Horseboy!"

Like toddlers who had discovered a new word, many of the kids around him started chanting, "Horse-boy, Horse-boy, Horse-boy," neighing and cackling viciously while the others stood there watching.

Jamie felt a surge of rage rise through his body like a jolt of electricity. A convulsion in his stomach made him sick. He hated them, he hated them all! It was not what they were calling him that hurt—he didn't care what they said—it was how they were ganging up against him; it was the vicious fun they were all having. There was a mindless cruelty in what they were doing that he couldn't come to grips with. He wanted to punch them, to kick them, to lash out at them, but he couldn't focus his anger on anybody, because they were all bouncing the taunting around. He felt the tears welling up again in his throat. He didn't want to cry in front of this pack of fiends.

"Watchya gonna do? You gonna cry now, Horseboy?" Luka called out.

Jamie zeroed in on him. "Shut up!" he growled and rushed at him.

Luka bolted forward and shoved him over. "Oh yeah, and what you gonna do about it, Hors—"

Jamie snarled and threw a shattering punch straight into his stomach. Luka went white and froze.

Jamie's fury subsided instantly and he started worrying Luka would punch him back. Instead, he muttered something about the restroom and sneaked away, clutching his stomach.

All the kids around stopped their taunting as mindlessly as they had started. Silence fell in the hall like a lead curtain.

Jamie stood rooted to the spot, dazed. It was the first time he had punched anybody and he was confused. It had felt good and the right thing to do, but he had hurt somebody and that made him uncomfortable. He was still thinking about it when he felt the strong hand of an adult clamp hard around his arm.

"What do you think you're doing, boy!?" a male voice growled.

Jamie looked up. Mr. Culvert was glowering down at him, his face contorted with fury.

He blinked stupidly at the principal. His brain jammed, blinded by white panic. All he could think about was that he didn't want to be expelled.

Mr. Culvert dragged him bodily to his office and slammed the door behind him. He dropped him onto a green, fake leather couch, while he went and sat behind his bulky dark wooden desk.

Jamie rubbed his nose. The whole place smelled of incense and strong cologne. He felt he was in the back room of some church and not in a principal's office.

Mr. Culvert was a gray man in his fifties who dressed as if he was in the seventies. He was wearing a horrible gray suit with a loud patterned shirt and a dark green tie. He had gray hair and gray skin and an air of ash and dust around him. Jamie always compared him to a moth, a very religious moth with horrible taste in clothing—he always wore the cross and preached to them whenever he could.

Jamie stared at him, trying desperately to think about something to say. He needed to explain to him that it wasn't his fault.

"Jamie," Mr. Culvert said coldly, gathering some paper on his desk, "your behavior really disappoints me."

"But Mr. Culvert, he—"

"I don't want to hear any excuses!" he cut in, raising his voice.

Jamie winced. "But it's not my fault. They were all calling me—"

"Silence!" Mr. Culvert shouted, slamming the desk hard with the palm of his hand.

A deafening crack boomed in Jamie's ears. He froze, petrified.

"Violence is wrong, young man, and I will not allow it in my school! If somebody was bothering you, you should have called Ms. Ambrose or me."

Jamie came back to his senses. As if that would have helped, he thought . She'd have joined in, he was sure. His eyes narrowed, weighing Mr. Culvert. There it was—somebody else who didn't know what he was talking about. In a split second, he lost all respect for this man who was supposed to be the principal of his school.

"For this time, I will be lenient," Mr. Culvert said. "You'll just get detention here in the office until class ends." He scribbled something on a piece of paper and handed it to him. "I want you to copy this until the message is clear in your mind."

Jamie glanced at the paper. It read:

If someone strikes me on the right cheek, I will turn to him the other also.

A wry smile twitched at the corner his lips. He gazed up into Mr. Culvert's gray eyes and realized this man didn't care at all about him. He didn't care he had been bullied or that he was innocent. He didn't even want to find out. All he cared about was a stock phrase and that was it. His mother was right, Mr. Culvert didn't deserve the chair he was sitting on.

He took the piece of paper without a word and started writing. At least he didn't have to be in class.

When the bell rang an hour and a half later, Jamie raised his head from the paper. With a groan of pain, he opened his hand. His cramping fingers let out a series of ominous cracking sounds, then the pen he had been holding for so long finally slid onto the desk. He massaged his hand and sighed—the torture was over.

He picked up the paper and dropped it together with the rest on the stack in front of Mr. Culvert. The thick layer of sheets was crammed ceaselessly with the monotonous drone of the phrase:

If someone strikes me on the right cheek, I will turn to him the other also.

Jamie felt drained as if his brain had been pulled out through his nostrils. The message had sunken in deep, he thought—just not in the way Mr. Culvert had wanted it to. Now he was absolutely sure he had done the right thing in punching Luka. Mr. Culvert could turn his ugly cheek also if he liked it so much, but he wasn't going to let people hurt him without defending himself.

"You can go now," Mr. Culvert said, gathering his things.

Jamie stood up. "Have a good day, Sir." He wished somebody ran him over.

Mr. Culvert frowned.

Jamie spun on his heels. He strode out of the office and headed back to his classroom. The throng of his classmates rushing in the opposite direction parted like the Red Sea before him, avoiding any contact. Jamie was grateful that they were leaving him alone.

He walked into the room and noticed that his essay was back on the table. He was sure he had stuffed it in his backpack before going out. His classmates must have pulled it out to spite him.

As he stepped closer, he caught sight of the drawing on the paper and the little warmth that was left in him seeped away. Crudely traced in blue ink on the center of the page was a sketch of a horse and a kid laced together in a lewd French kiss. Below it, in capital letters, was the phrase:

GO BACK TO YOUR FARM, HORSEBOY!

The rest of the paper was littered with scribbles that repeated ceaselessly the words horseboy and snitch in different colors and handwriting. It was obvious his classmates had passed the paper around. It had been a group project.

So they were actually not going to leave him alone. A wave of despair washed over him. He felt powerless, targeted, punished for no good reason at all. He felt again as if a mob of stray dogs were circling him, tearing him to pieces one bit at a time.

He wrenched his eyes away from the drawing and shoved the piece of paper back into his backpack. Why were they doing this to him? A hoarse rush of anger hit his throat with a nasty throb. He needed to get away as quickly as possible. He wasn't coming back tomorrow. He'd find an excuse—that he felt ill or something. He couldn't come back.

He threw his backpack on his shoulders and marched out of the room. He took the corridor that led to the back of the school and pushed open the metal door. As he walked outside in the sun, he looked for his bike—it was still there. Thank goodness.

Suddenly he heard the sound of feet sprinting toward him. He wheeled around and caught a glance of Luka throwing up his foot at him. He braced himself as Luka's foot drove into his stomach and shoved him over.

He crashed against his own bike and toppled over. A sharp pain cracked through his right knee as he hit the ground, floundering. He tried to pull himself up, but his knee gave way. He glanced up and suddenly realized Luka was not alone. Simon Perk and four boys he didn't know fanned out and closed in.

They were going to beat him up, Jamie thought with dread. So this was his payback for punching Luka. How brave of him to take his whole gang against him.

"Hello, Horseboy!" Luka called, and immediately he spit in his face.

A fleck of saliva hit Jamie's cheek. Hurriedly, he wiped it off, but before he could finish, the other boys had started spitting at him too. Jamie tried to dodge, but they surrounded him. He tried to stand up, but they tripped him and kicked him back down.

He couldn't see while they were spitting in his face. He flailed his limbs desperately at them, trying to hit them, to kick them, but they kept out of reach, spitting and cackling and chanting, "Horse-boy, Horse-boy, Horse-boy, Horse-boy," over and over again.

Jamie felt wet lumps of saliva splat on his face and arms—warm and sticky and heavy with shame. His skin flared up at the contact as if it were acid. His ears were filled with the cackling and catcalls of the boys. He thought he was going to lose his mind. He didn't want to be spit all over—this was even worse than being beaten up.

He felt as if he had fallen into a pit. Everything around him became distant and muffled. He stopped trying to protect his face and let his head down. It didn't matter they were spitting on him. None of this made any sense. It didn't matter. Tears rolled up in the back of his throat.

As suddenly as a summer rainstorm, the spitting subsided.

"Yeah, go home and cry to your horsey, Horseboy!" Luka sneered. The others let out a final roar of laughter, then they ran away.

Jamie watched their sneakers leave his field of vision. Their voices faded in the distance. It's over, he thought. Get up. He gave the command to his body, but instead his mouth filled with a sickening sweet taste. His limbs felt as if warm glue had been injected through his veins. Standing there on the ground, slowly drifting into oblivion felt good. Get up! he shouted in his head. He hated that sick sensation. Get up!!

At length, his body responded. Jamie struggled to his feet and limped to his bike. He pulled up the inside of his T-shirt and wiped the spit from his face as best as he could. He needed to get away from there. He didn't dare look up for fear of meeting the gaze of an onlooker. He mounted on his bike despite the sharp pain in his knee and pedaled away at full speed.

14
──────

SHAME

The buildings flashed by, then the fields. Jamie thought his knee was going to split apart, but he didn't want to slow down, nor to stop. He must get home.

He felt the air rushing at him and dry in a thin shell the wet layer of saliva on his face and scalp. His skin stretched and started prickling. To think that just a few days ago he had told himself that spit was nothing. A groan of disgust escaped his lips. He clenched his fists around the handles of his bike and pressed harder on his aching knee.

He shouldn't have challenged Luka, he shouldn't have written that stupid essay, he shouldn't have talked to his mom. He should have kept quiet and all this would not have happened. Why was he so dumb? Why!?

If he could, he would have deserted himself then and there. But he couldn't; he had to live with himself. He hated that.

Finally, the woods swallowed him in their dark shade. Jamie caught a glimpse of his home and slowed down, catching his breath. He let the bike glide idly down the slope and stopped in front of the gate. He didn't know what to do next.

Tentatively, he turned the lock, hoping his mom wouldn't be

outside. She wasn't. Half-relieved, half-disappointed, he parked his bike against the wall of the house. He noticed the strange confusion of his feelings and didn't know what to make of it. He didn't want to bump into his mom. Perhaps, he could manage to sneak upstairs and take a shower before she caught sight of him. He opened the wooden door of the living room. The stone floor seized his feet in a cold grip as it always did.

"Hey, baby," Maddie called from the kitchen.

He should run now, Jamie thought, but he hesitated. He heard her footsteps approaching. He wanted her to see him, he realized. He wanted her to stop the pain, to wash him, to wash away the spit, to wash away the shame, because he couldn't do it by himself. He suddenly felt like a crybaby who needed mommy to make his boo-boo go away. The urge to hide mounted back inside him, but it was too late—she was already emerging from the doorway.

"Go wash your hands, tig..." The words died on Maddie's lips as she saw him. Her cheerfulness turned into shock. She ran up to him and kneeled down. "Are you OK? What happened?"

Jamie looked away. Now that he was actually faced with the prospect of telling her, he balked. He didn't want to talk to her, yet he wanted nothing better than that. He struggled with himself. If he kept quiet, maybe things would go away, maybe people would forget and things would go back to normal. Maybe... But there was an unbearable pressure inside him, a flood of anger, frustration and shame that clashed with that restraint. He hadn't done anything wrong, so why should he be afraid of speaking out? People were hurting him, so why should he stand that in silence?

"They spit on me because I wrote Acorn is my best friend," he said, staring at his feet. He immediately regretted it. He felt like a coward. Go home and cry to mommy, just as Luka had said. He was weak. If he hadn't been, they wouldn't have attacked him. Just like stray dogs... They had seen he was weak and they were out to destroy him. How could he prevent that? Why couldn't he see his own weakness? Was he too... weird? The word came into his mind with a shudder. Was he weird? Too weird to even see how strange he was? Was that why they were attacking him?

"Who spit on you?" Maddie asked.

Jamie startled. He couldn't take it back anymore. "It was Luka."

"Luka who?"

"Luka Gassner. And Simon Perk—they're always together—and four other boys I don't know."

Maddie gasped. "It was six against one?"

Jamie shrugged. What difference did it make? He just wanted to forget about it.

"Why did they do it? What happened?"

"I read my essay in class and they started making fun of me —my classmates. And Luka, he called me Horseboy and they all imitated him. I punched Luka, then Mr. Culvert gave me detention and stupid lines to write." The words rolled out of his mouth like dead slugs.

Maddie's eyes narrowed. "What was it about?"

Jamie blinked. "I... I punched Luka because he—"

Maddie waved her hand. "No, what was the essay about?"

"Oh..." Jamie lowered his eyes. "My best friend. We needed to write about our best friend. I wrote about Acorn. Everybody else was being mean to me. I was angry at them."

Maddie frowned. "And Ms. Ambrose made you read it aloud in class?"

Jamie nodded.

She held out her hand. "Can I see it?"

He winced.

"What's wrong?"

"Nothing..." He didn't want her to see the drawing. "Can I show it to you later?"

Maddie's worried frown deepened. "No, I want to see it now."

Jamie flushed. He took off his backpack and pulled the zip open. He spotted the essay sandwiched between two of his books. He pulled it out slowly, hoping in vain that it could self-destruct at the count of five like in spy movies. Why did he even keep it? He should have torn it to shreds.

Maddie pried the essay from his clasped fingers. Her gaze hardened into an appalled glare at the sight of the obscene drawing. "Who did this?"

"I don't know. It was like that when I came back after detention."

Maddie's eyes roved feverishly over the paper.

Jamie saw her stare at the big red C that soiled the top corner of his essay and he blushed. "She gave me a C because she said I didn't do the assignment."

Maddie tore her eyes off the drawing, the scribbles, the insults, and looked up at him. "How so?"

"She said pets aren't people. And that you keep me locked up in the farm too much if I think they are."

Maddie snorted. "I see." The corners of her mouth twisted down in a grimace of disgust. Suddenly, a wild look came upon her face and she bolted upright. "Let's go!" She grabbed Jamie by the arm and pulled him toward the door.

He dug his heels, panicking. "Why? Where are we going?"

"To Ms. Ambrose!"

"No," he said frantically, "she didn't do anything this time."

"She didn't do anything!?" Maddie snarled, turning on him.

Jamie flinched.

She checked herself at the look of panic on his face and kneeled down. "She set your classmates on you, Jamie. Do you understand? That's what she did. It's her fault this happened."

"But, she just made me read the essay in class."

"Exactly. And she humiliated you in front of them, saying you hadn't done the assignment. And made that snide remark that you were crazy for being friends with a horse."

He didn't reply, unable to make heads or tails of all that was happening around him.

Maddie stood up again. "Piece of scum. She thinks she's sly setting your classmates against you after I told her not to touch you."

Jamie didn't want to go. He wanted his mom to take care of it and come back telling him that everything was all right, that she had faced everything, that he could wash himself, that the shame would come off. But he was too mystified by the awful things that were happening to muster the strength to protest. He let her stuff him into the car and drive him away.

As Thelma lurched precariously toward Ms. Ambrose's house, he felt trapped in a nightmare that kept repeating itself, tossed around like a doll, powerless. He mulled over what his mom had said, incredulous at his own stupidity. Why didn't he realize Ms. Ambrose had done it on purpose? It was so obvious. She was always two steps ahead of him. At this rate, she was going to wrap him around her finger any way she pleased. He wished with all his might he could be smarter—he desperately needed to.

On the other hand, if what his mom said was true and she was able to stop Ms. Ambrose, then everything else would stop, the pain would stop. But how was she going to do that? She had already talked to Ms. Ambrose once and that had not stopped her at all. What did she have in mind this time? His stomach squirmed uncomfortably as a presentiment struck him.

Maddie pulled off next to a house he didn't know. He examined the building. It was some kind of villa—it looked expensive. He had no idea teachers made so much money that they could afford a place like that. Maybe his mom should have been a teacher too, he thought. The architecture of the building was nice, but there was something wrong with it. Perhaps the lack of color? It was all shades of gray and maroon. Only the hedge gave a touch of liveliness to the scene, but it was one of those perfectly trimmed, too-tidy-to-be-real kind of affairs that he couldn't stand. Why have a plant in your garden if you made it look like a piece of furniture? The whole place had that same too-neat, too-well-kept air that made him uncomfortable. Maybe it was just because it was Ms. Ambrose's house, but he didn't like it.

Maddie pulled him out of the car.

As they marched toward the front door, a sense of impending doom filled Jamie like a sinking ship.

Maddie rang the bell.

He turned around and noticed that a few of the neighbors were out in their gardens or in the street.

As someone approached on the other side of the door, the sound of clicking heels grew louder. The person stopped and opened the peephole, then closed it again. There was a pause, silence, then the door opened.

Ms. Ambrose appeared in the doorframe. Her face didn't betray any emotions. "Yes?"

Jamie felt his mom stiffen like a board, then she pulled him in front of her and did exactly what he had dreaded: she started screaming.

"Are you happy now!?" Her voice was clear and carried a long way.

Jamie had the impression she was doing it on purpose. He turned around and saw some of the neighbors raise their heads and look their way.

"Excuse me?" Ms. Ambrose replied.

Maddie made a swiping gesture toward Jamie. "Some of your

students spit on my son because you made fun of him in front of them!"

"There is no need to shout. I can hear you perfectly well from where I stand."

Maddie ignored her. "What do you have to say!?"

Ms. Ambrose raised her brow and surveyed Jamie.

He glanced up at her. Certainly she didn't look appalled at seeing him covered in spit. There was no pity in her eyes, no sympathy, nothing. She could very well be looking at a stone.

"Who did that?"

"This kid Luka," answered Maddie.

Ms. Ambrose raised her eyebrow. "Jamie punched Luka in the hallway. It was probably payback for that. It has nothing to do with me."

"I already told you once, woman," Maddie hissed poisonously. "Do not play me for a fool! I'm not a kid you can wrap around your finger!"

Ms. Ambrose flinched. She straightened up and made to close the door. "I don't have to stay here and stand your gratuitous abuse. Good day, Mrs.—"

Maddie grabbed hold of the door. "It has nothing to do with you? You gave my son a C, told him he hadn't done the assignment and then proceeded to make fun of him in front of all his classmates. And you want to tell me that has nothing to do with you?"

"He was supposed to write about a person," Ms. Ambrose replied flatly. "It says people in the guidelines, persons—you can check. Horses aren't people."

"He could have written about a mattress for all I care. You don't go and mortify a kid in front of all his peers. What kind of a person are you?"

Ms. Ambrose's face twisted into a nasty smile. "I'm sure, Mrs. Blackshear, that as mothers we both share the same desire for

Jamie to have healthy interpersonal relationships. What happened is really unfortunate, but you can't—"

Maddie pushed Jamie aside and stepped forward. "I assure you, Ms. Ambrose, that there isn't anything at all we share. You think I don't know what you're doing? I am warning you one last time. Don't you ever dare to embarrass my son in front of his classmates ever again!"

Ms. Ambrose's eyes narrowed to two dirty slits. "Are you threatening me?"

Maddie sneered. "We're past threats, darling. Watch your back!"

Jamie saw Ms. Ambrose open her mouth to reply, but his mom grabbed him and wheeled him around. He heard the door slam behind him and, before he knew it, they were marching back to the car.

He saw the neighbors in the street crane their necks trying to get a better look at him. He felt his mom's hand holding him in front of her as if he were a thing, a piece of evidence that was being shown to the jury: here is the poor boy Jamie who can't defend himself —check out the spit all over his face and clothes. He flushed and stared at the ground. He wished those people would look away. He wished his mom hadn't screamed on purpose to get their attention. He wished he could sink through the pavement and disappear from the face of the Earth.

As soon as he got into the car, he tucked down out of view, making himself as small as he could. He looked up at his mother and saw she was shaking with fury, but there was also a faint smile on her lips as if she was satisfied about something. Outside of the car window, Ms. Ambrose's house glided away mercifully.

So that was it, he thought. That was how she was going to stop Ms. Ambrose: by screaming at her.

"We had to do it, Jamie," Maddie said, glancing at him.

He frowned.

"Now she can't deny what happened. That you've been spit on. We have witnesses. She's been warned—she knows she can't fool us anymore."

Great, really great, he thought. So she had shown him around all covered in spit as if he was a freak just to tell Ms. Ambrose off. Just to make a point. Great...

Anger mounted inside him, swirling and all consuming. He had wanted his mom to come to his rescue, so it was his fault all this happened. He should have known better. He should have kept his mouth shut. Things and thoughts and faces floated in front of his eyes—fuzzy, blazing, spinning out of control. He felt the unbearable urge to sleep, to forget.

The vile film of scum on his skin started prickling again. He wished he could peel it off like onion skin without feeling like crying.

15

ALONE

As soon as they got home, Maddie rushed to the phone. Jamie didn't want to be in the room for another shouting match. He had no idea who she wanted to call, but he was sure it was going to be nasty. He climbed the stairs and hid in the bathroom.

He locked the door and stared at the shower. Just a few days ago, he had told himself that spit comes off, but now he wasn't so sure anymore. Were water and soap going to be enough to scrub away the shame? It was almost better to keep it on than to risk washing and not see it come off. What if it had seeped through his skin and nested itself there, how was he ever going to get rid of it? Maybe it was too late already.

Through the closed door, he heard his mom climb the stairs. A burst of anger flared up in his chest. He didn't want to talk to her anymore; he didn't want her to wash him anymore. He sprang to the shower and cranked the hot water open all the way, then froze, still as a statue.

"Jamie!" Maddie called from behind the door.

He didn't move a finger, pretending he couldn't hear her.

There was a moment of silence, then a knock. "Jamie..."

He turned and stared at the closed door. He heard the shuffling of her feet, then her steps faded out of earshot. He unglued his eyes from the wooden door and watched the hot water spraying out of the shower head. The vapor billowed toward him in quick swirls. He breathed in the familiar and comforting smell. Maybe taking a shower would work, after all.

He peeled off his clothes and stepped under the shower head, letting the water fill his ears, drowning all outside sounds. He picked up his shampoo and lathered his head in foam. Everything became soft and squishy and warm under his fingers. He poured more shampoo and then sealed his whole body in soap. Through the cheap plastic shower curtain, his uncertain shape looked like that of a larva turning over in its own cocoon.

He stood covered in foam for a moment as the water hit the curtain at his side and streamed away at his feet. He imagined the soap bubbles on his skin slowly and methodically sucking up the filth and sealing it inside their round bodies, just like white cells he had once seen in a documentary on TV. He sighed and stepped under the jet of water. The foam glided away, dragging the dirt into the darkness of the drain below.

A faint sense of relief started getting hold of him. A pet is not a person, Ms. Ambrose's voice echoed in his mind. He grimaced —he knew he was supposed to write about a person and he also knew that animals were not people, but he realized the thought had not occurred to him that Acorn could not be a person. He saw no difference between Acorn and his classmates, apart from the fact that he was of another species. I mean, he was different, but Acorn had a personality, he was a person. At least to him. Was that... weird? His mom thought it was fine, but then all his classmates had laughed at him as if he were crazy. And Ms. Ambrose—a shudder ran up his spine at the thought—if what he thought was normal, how could she use it against him? To be

a weapon it must be something negative, no? So, it was weird...
He was weird. Was that why...?

He had to know.

He turned off the water and stepped out of the shower. His
skin felt hot and his muscles lax, weak, despite the tension
inside him. He listened for a second for any telltale sound of his
mom. Beyond the door, everything was silent—the way was
clear.

He tied a towel around his waist and peeked out, then
tiptoed into his parents' bedroom. As usual, they had forgotten
the bulky cordless phone on the bedside table.

He picked it up and crept back silently into the bathroom.
He locked the door and sat on the toilet. He felt the rough fabric
of the wet towel press against his naked thighs while the cold
ceramic of the bowl brushed against the back of his knees. He
dialed the number. The warmth clinging on the surface of his
wet skin slowly dissipated through the air. He waited, then the
phone started ringing on the other end of the line. Somebody
picked up.

"Hello?" came Mrs. Roeg's voice from the receiver.

An inarticulate sound escaped his lips. He quickly cleared
his throat—blushing in the desert bathroom—and said more
clearly, "Hello, Mrs. Roeg, this is Jamie."

"Oh, hello dear."

"May I talk to Holly, please?"

"Yes, of course. Hold on."

He heard her walking away. She sounded relaxed—Holly
must not have told her what happened. He was thankful. He
liked Mrs. Roeg and didn't want to look like a fool in her eyes. He
heard a pair of lighter steps approach the phone and felt his
cheeks flush. Thankfully, Holly couldn't see him.

"Hey," came Holly's voice through the receiver.

"Hey... How's it going?"

"Math's killing me, you know."

"Yeah, you're always behind..."

"Right... Do you need the list of homework assignments?"

He braced himself. "No, I didn't call for that."

"Oh..."

He had the impression he could hear Holly's body stiffen. He couldn't turn back though, so he said all at once, "Holly, do you think I'm weird?"

The line fell silent. He could hear only white noise over his own breathing. "That's why you never want to—"

"I... I've got to go."

The line clicked off.

"—see me..." The words lingered in the room like the carcass of an abandoned animal.

From the receiver in his hand came the rhythmic buzzing of a busy line. He clicked the off button and laid the useless plastic instrument in his lap.

So that was what they were all running away from: him. He was weird. They all thought he was weird.

Horseboy! The jeer echoed in his mind. Why could he not just have another kid as best friend? He liked people, he liked people! Why did he have to be lonely?

Anger clawed at his throat. If he hadn't grown up with a horse, he'd have friends now! Why didn't his mom stop that? She knew people would make fun of him. She must know. What was wrong with her? Why hadn't she protected him? Now he was never going to have friends for the rest of his life. How was he going to ever make himself normal now? Was there a cure for weirdness, a shot or something he could take? Or would he just have to hide in shame for good?

Suddenly he felt a silent wave run through his limbs. His mouth started filling with a sickening sweet taste. His body longed for immobility; his soul longed for it too. He hated that

feeling—it terrified him. Move! His feet hurt. He suddenly realized he was cold; his feet almost numb. Move, he ordered
himself. Move!!

He jumped up, his head spinning. He staggered to the door
and went into his room. He threw the wet towel on the bed. He
was freezing, his skin all wrinkled up with goose bumps. The
cold made him shiver and brought him back to his senses. He
caught a glance of his naked body in the mirror of the closet and
looked away disgusted.

He put on the first pair of jeans he found lying around, a
shirt, then slipped into his sneakers. He knew Mom was waiting
for him downstairs. This time, he was sure he wanted to
avoid her.

He tiptoed to the sliding glass door in his bedroom. Trying to
make as little noise as possible, he turned the metal knob. The
door squeaked and opened. He listened for telltale sounds in the
kitchen below, then stepped out.

He walked to the far east corner of the balcony, away from
the kitchen, straddled over the balustrade and lowered himself.
He knew he could jump—he had tested himself—but today his
body felt like a remote place, so he needed to be more careful.
He climbed down until he was able to suspend himself with his
hands from the cement pavement of the parapet. He was only a
couple of feet from the ground now. He hung in midair for a
second, then let go and landed silently in the grass.

"Jamie!"

He gave a start and wheeled around. His mom stood a few
feet from him, holding his crumpled essay in her hand. She had
been waiting for him—she knew him too well.

She walked up to him and kneeled down, getting hold of his
arm. "Jamie, this is wonderful," she said, holding up his paper.
"There isn't anything to be ashamed of."

Oh yes, there is plenty to be ashamed of, he thought with spite. "Can I go now?"

"Kitten..."

He looked away. He didn't want to talk to her anymore; he didn't trust her anymore. She had made a fool of him in front of other people for no good reason. She had let him be friends with a horse, knowing that others would make fun of him. She should have protected him!

Maddie bit her lip.

He felt her hand brush his head, the warmth of her skin on his, but this time it didn't give him comfort. On the contrary, it made him feel even more fretful and annoyed. He pulled away from her clutch.

Maddie let go of him, a pained look strained across her face.

He turned around and walked to the back of the house. His body felt soggy, slow. The longing for immobility still lingered somewhere in his blood. He needed to do something.

He scuffed to the nook where his scruffy mini basketball was hidden and pulled it out. He shuffled it tentatively in his hands a couple of times, then started bouncing it. The saggy ball lazily slapped the ground. He threw it down with more conviction. The blood started pumping faster in his veins. He felt a burst of adrenaline rush through him with a shiver. A second later, the sensation was gone, drowned in the flaccid, glue-like anguish that pervaded him.

From around the corner, Acorn peeked in, his ears pricked up in excitement.

Jamie saw Acorn's cheerful face and bile rose to his mouth. Why was he always so freaking happy? Dumb horse. There was nothing to be happy about. "Not now," he grumbled.

Acorn was too excited to listen to him. He trotted in and placed himself in front of the hoop.

Something reared up inside Jamie. "Why don't you ever listen to me!" he suddenly yelled at the top of his lungs.

Acorn startled.

A surge of rage blazed through Jamie. What the hell did this horse want with him? Why wasn't it best friends with another horse or a goat instead of him? It was weird, not him! And it had passed on his weirdness to him like a disease. He didn't want to be weird. It was all its fault, all its fault! Point blank, he flung the ball.

The rubber bullet slapped hard against Acorn's neck, making him flinch.

The ball rolled back limply toward Jamie's feet. He picked it up. It was all its fault! All its fault, screamed his mind. Why did it want to play with him? He wasn't a horse! He wound up and flung the ball again with all his might.

Acorn braced himself. The basketball hit his flank with a loud smack that echoed against the trees.

"Didn't you hear me!?" Jamie shouted, flecks of spit flying from his mouth. "Get out of my face! Get out! Get out!!"

Acorn shied away. He pulled his ears back, bared his teeth toward him, then galloped away.

Jamie watched him go and sneered. It served it right, he thought. He bent down to pick up the ball and his knees buckled. He straightened up jerkily and realized his whole body was shaking uncontrollably. He raised his trembling hands to his eyes and ordered himself to calm down. Now that he had let it out, the anger was flooding him, taking over. He felt the unbearable urge to throw the ball again, to throw it until he smashed it.

He picked it up and with a snarl flung it against the wall. A red flare burst in front of his eyes and the rage ramped up a knot. He panicked, terrified by this overwhelming sensation that only seemed to grow larger and more violent the more he let it out. He felt he was losing his mind. He wanted to stop shaking.

He again ordered himself to calm down, unclenched his teeth with difficulty and drew in a painful gasp. His belabored breathing slowed down. He took a few more breaths and the red fog enveloping him started clearing up.

A new thought surfaced in his mind. With a cold sense of dread, he realized that he had just alienated the only creature apart from his mom who still wanted to be around him. A loneliness even worse than what he had felt so far closed in on him. The raging fire inside him extinguished, choked by sticky, bitter anguish.

He felt cheated: he had been given only losing cards. What was he supposed to do now? Make peace with Acorn? Yet, what other choice did he have, unless he wanted to be completely alone? At least until he figured out whether he could somehow win his friends back, he better bite the bullet. With a snort of disgust, he kicked the ball aside and halfheartedly made his way toward the stables.

He trudged to Acorn's box and saw him hidden in a dark corner, tense and upset. He lowered his gaze and leaned against the door.

Acorn retreated even farther into the shadows, but Jamie didn't notice.

"Looks like I'm stuck with you," he grumbled, looking up.

Their eyes met.

Acorn jolted back, panicking. He knocked against the inner wall of the box with a booming crash, then reared and bolted forward.

Jamie gave a start and tried to jump out of the way. Too late. Acorn's chest drove into his at full speed and flung him out of the box, then all the air exploded out of his lungs as his back crashed against the concrete pavement. Out of the corner of his eye, he saw the metal of Acorn's horseshoes hit the ground only a foot from his head, sending sparks flying onto his cheeks, then Acorn rushed past and disappeared into the paddock.

He doubled up on the dirty pavement, moaning in pain. His chest burned like a furnace, shattered by a blow that was still ringing through his whole body. He gasped, but his throat had seized and would not let air in. He was choking! He commanded himself to freeze, stay calm, relax his muscles. His head started spinning for lack of air, then finally his throat unclenched. He drew in a painful wheeze. The feeling came back into his numb chest and with it a flood of pain. The stab at the mouth of his stomach was so intense that he started gagging. Cold sweat slathered his back as he struggled to breathe without vomiting.

The pain was atrocious—not just the pain in his chest and his back, but that in his heart, his mind, his soul. What had he done? He had never seen Acorn like that—he was terrified of him. He must have caught sight of the rage, the contempt deep inside him. He felt ashamed of himself. He wanted to cry, but his eyes were dry, parched.

He dragged up his leaden body and made his way back home. There was nothing to be done with Acorn, at least not now. Before he could get closer to him again, he knew he needed to get rid of his anger. How long would that take, he didn't know. Better not think about it.

He pushed open the creaking wicket that lead into the garden and spotted his father's car in the driveway. Blood froze in his veins. He hoped his mom had not ratted on him.

He tiptoed stealthily toward the kitchen door, making sure to keep out of sight. He leaned against the wall and listened. If his parents were in the kitchen, he was ready to climb up to the balcony and sneak into his room through their bedroom.

He stretched his ears, but couldn't hear anything. Cautiously, he made his way inside. Everything was still. He shuffled through the living room as quietly as he could and reached the stairs. The muffled voices of his parents filtered down to him. They must be in their bedroom, he thought. If he was quick, he could hide inside his room.

In the utmost silence, he started climbing two steps at a time. Slowly and carefully, he made his way closer to his door. He could hear his own breathing as loud as a locomotive in his ears, but hopefully it was too quiet for his parents to hear through the closed door of their room.

His right knee suddenly popped. He froze. The chatting in his parents' bedroom continued uninterrupted. He resumed climbing.

He reached his room and was about to turn the knob, when he heard his father's voice through the closed door of their bedroom.

"You never should have allowed him to spend so much time with that horse!"

Jamie swallowed. They were talking about him. He wanted to turn away and go lie down on his bed, away from all the pain, but he felt the urge to know what his parents were saying—he had been backstabbed enough.

"Don't say that," came Maddie's voice. "You know how much he loves Acorn."

Jamie tiptoed toward the door and leaned in.

"He treats it like a person," his father said. "That's not normal. Of course he doesn't have friends. Why can't he be like all the other boys and just play football? He's turning into a fairy. I told you he needs to get a job and man up. He didn't even defend himself when they spit all over him!"

He had defended himself, Jamie protested in his mind. At least he had tried to.

"It was six against one, Jan!" Maddie replied.

"So what? He should have at least sacked one. Stand up for himself!"

The bile in his father's voice made his stomach lurch. It was six against one. What did he want him to do? Did he need him to get killed to make him happy? Or to kill somebody? Was that what he wanted? He always showed off as if he was superman, so why didn't he go now and teach a lesson to those six instead of yapping insults at him?

"That kid is such a failure!" Jan barked through the closed door.

Jamie's temper rose. He slammed the door open. "That's why I despise you!" he shouted in his face.

Jan goggled at him, stunned.

Jamie smelled the stench of alcohol in his breath, as vile as his words. He spun around and rushed into his bedroom, then locked himself in and sat on his bed, shaking with fury. He heard his mom run at the door and turn the knob. The door wobbled and clunked loudly.

"Jamie, kitten, are you all right?"

He didn't answer and slid under the bed covers still dressed.

"Baby, you know that he doesn't mean it."

"Oh yes, he did mean it!" he snarled. And she hadn't said anything to defend him. Nobody had since this whole thing had started. He hated them, he hated them all!

The sweet, nauseating tide slowly surged again through his blood. This time, he didn't fight it back. He let it come over and swallow him. Before he sunk into a black, dreamless abyss, he was briefly aware of some wetness on his cheeks. Tears, he thought. Who cares...

16

STICKS AND STONES

The days passed like broken toy records. They skipped, repeated themselves, made no sense at all, and left Jamie with a vague feeling of confusion and emptiness.

At school, he tried his best to lie low. It worked too well: not a soul talked to him. He sat alone, ate alone, played alone. A deep melancholy enveloped him like a cloak. He walked in misery with his eyes stuck to the ground, trying to forget his problems, to forget himself, so maybe everybody else would forget too.

At home, he avoided his mom and Acorn, sneaking around like a thief in his own house. He was still angry at her for not having defended him in front of his father and for having humiliated him. Strangely, she hadn't sat him down and forced him to talk as she usually did. Maybe she felt guilty, because she seemed to avoid him too. He didn't want to speak to her, but wished nevertheless that she would apologize. He might be able to forgive her then—he missed her.

As for Acorn, he was ashamed of how he had treated him, but he couldn't bring himself to do anything about it. Perhaps it was better this way, because he was sure that if he wanted to be around people, they couldn't be together anymore. He struggled with the idea of a life without Acorn. Every day without him felt like an empty box with no present. He missed him terribly, even though he knew that missing a horse as if it was a person was wrong. But if being friends with a horse was going to condemn him to loneliness, then he needed to change. He wanted friends —he liked people. He just needed to make people like him back. Nevertheless, he kept wondering if what he was trading Acorn's friendship for was worth it.

He raised his eyes to the sky—the day was cloudy and gray.

A week had passed since the spitting party. A whole week, he thought, dazed by the unrelenting marching of time. He felt a vague sense of loss in the pit of his stomach—so many sunny days lost, so much happiness gone.

He took off his shoes and waded in the water. He pushed some reeds aside and tried to find a viable path through the cane thicket. He shivered as the water crawled up above his knees—it was still way too early for a swim in the lake. He picked up his toy telescope from his pocket and held it in his hand so that it wouldn't get wet.

He trudged forward carefully, his eyes searching for signs of suspicious movement. He was always afraid of bumping into a water snake out hunting for prey. Those things were too fast on water and they could bite a hole in you. It was more likely that it would swim away if it saw him, but if you caught one unawares, there was no telling what it would do. It was the same with any animal really—you just had to be careful or pay the price for your foolishness. He was glad animals usually liked him. Usually, he thought with pain, remembering Acorn's panicked look and the violence of his reaction.

He shook his head, trying to wipe away the awful memory. He recognized the gnarled tree ahead, rising among the mass of reeds—almost there. For sure he could have made his life easier and get directly at it from the shore, since it stood only ten feet away from the edge of the water. That way, though, he would have opened a trail that other people could follow. That would have been foolish—it would have put his treasure up for plunder.

He struggled forward, paying attention not to step with his bare feet on the sharp ends of underwater stubs. The hollow gash in the tree trunk came into view.

He extracted himself from the thicket and stood in the small clearing. The tree rested on a single patch of land that emerged from the water. Its roots clutched deeply into the earth, giving it the appearance of a castaway holding for dear life to the island it had been stranded on. He wondered how long the old stump could stand in that precarious state before the earth slid from under its feet. Every time he came back, he expected to find it lying on its side, drowned dead. He was always pleasantly surprised to discover it still standing instead.

"How are you holding up today?" he said, patting the dark bark affectionately. That thing really was a miracle of stubbornness and resilience. He wished he could be as strong. His eyes slid down and caught sight of the chain fastened around the trunk. He felt a twitch of guilt—it was disheartening to see such a proud creature shackled with irons.

Come on, he told himself, it wasn't really like that!

He peeked around the tree and spotted the familiar outline of his treasure among the reeds on the other side of the clearing. The scuffed nose of his surfboard bobbed gently on the water, while its yellow body camouflaged perfectly with the golden brown of the cane thicket.

You see, he thought, it's your treasure that is in shackles, not the other way around. Still, he felt he should have some more respect and leave the old tree alone. It was probably having a hard time enough staying alive.

Who knew though. Maybe it was happy to help somebody else be free. After all, it knew the value of freedom and independence very well, since it was holding to it with all its might. For sure, he was grateful, deeply grateful to the tree for keeping his surfboard from being stolen, because it was his only means to explore the lake and enjoy the freedom of his excursions. Since the day last summer when he had found it drifting through the water lilies, he had thought of it as the greatest gift he had ever received—apart from Acorn, of course.

Jamie caught himself. Apart from Acorn, he repeated painfully in his mind. That time was gone.

He sighed and turned his thoughts back to his surfboard. He liked the battered old thing. It was like a rocket ship to him, a vehicle that could bring him where otherwise he couldn't have traveled. Sickly yellow and smeared with dirt and chipped and faded by the sun as it was, it was still gold to him.

He smiled in anticipation: it was time to take his treasure for a ride. He picked up some keys from his pocket and climbed up on the patch of earth held together by the tree's roots. He kneeled down, fit one of the keys in the padlock that fastened the noose around the trunk and uncoiled the chain.

He pulled and his surfboard wriggled out of the reeds, gliding eagerly toward him. As its nose knocked against the roots at his feet, he knelt down and patted it. "Good boy," he whispered, relishing the rough texture against his fingers. It made him think of the skin of a sea creature. He grinned—he liked to think of his treasure as a fish he could ride, a magical creature that had come to him in a time of need.

He unlocked the other padlock attached to the leash cup and freed it, then stood up and turned toward the tree. "Sorry, it'll be a second," he said politely, reaching inside the hollow of the trunk. He pulled out a makeshift paddle wrapped in a couple of plastic bags.

He had built it by fitting two hollow aluminum oars onto the wooden pole of a broken broom, and then securing everything together with a generous round of duct tape. The whole affair was ugly as sin, all brown, silver, black and pink-magenta, but it did the job and that was all he cared about really. Sometimes he was even proud of his craftiness when he traveled smoothly on the surface of the lake.

Trying not to make too much noise, he untied the bags and freed the paddle, then he wrapped the chain and hid everything inside the hollow trunk, out of sight. Finally ready to go, he mounted on his surfboard, crossed his legs, and paddled away.

Before emerging from the cane thicket, he made sure there was nobody around who could spot him and start wondering where he had come from. The coast clear, he glided silently into the open.

The lake was deserted. It was never very crowded, since it wasn't fit for swimming, but a rowing team usually trained there and in the spring there were campers paddling around in canoes and rubber boats. Today, though, nobody was around except for the birds. A red-necked grebe watched him warily as he paddled toward him, then plunged underwater and disappeared from view.

The large body of water was more like a vast pond than a lake, because it didn't have enough water supply from its tributaries to avoid becoming stagnant. Nevertheless, it was teeming with life. Plenty of fish, amphibians and birds had elected it their home.

He glided steadily toward the center of the lake, then veered right, pointing toward a thick stretch of reeds on the opposite shore.

The iron gray clouds reflected on the placid waters in an almost perfect mirror effect. Jamie had the impression of gliding on the sky, the illusion broken only by the rippling of his paddle.

He lifted his oars and let the momentum carry him forward on the glass-smooth water.

In the middle of the lake, everything was silent. Jamie felt calm, peaceful, almost happy. He took a deep breath and exhaled. He loved the water, probably as much as Acorn did...

Acorn again... He snorted. Would he ever stop thinking about him? He shook himself and tried to focus on the magnificence of the landscape. Why had happiness become something he could enjoy only in solitary excursions? Why had it become a slim event sandwiched between thick servings of unrelenting misery? Only a week ago life had still been good, so why? The answer came almost immediately, but he fought it: Acorn. One week ago, Acorn was still his best friend and with him at his side life had been a whole-day event, rich in surprises and adventures. Once again, he wondered if he was doing the right thing. Trading one friend for a million seemed like the right thing to do, but could you really trade a friend? Or could you only betray him?

Enough! He had come here to forget himself, to stop thinking about his troubles. Think about what's waiting for you, he told himself. The secret spot, think about the secret spot! It's not far now.

He reached the cane thicket near the shore and paddled along. After a few hundred yards, the reeds gave way to trees and bushes. He slowed down and studied the vegetation gliding by at his side. He spotted a narrow opening crammed between a bank covered in trees and a large bush that seemed to grow right out of the water. The passage was hardly big enough to let the surfboard through and it was almost impossible to see it unless you knew it was there. It was the gate to the secret spot, as he liked to refer to it.

Since it was too narrow to paddle, he grabbed a branch on his right and pulled himself through. Then he levered against the bank on his other side and pushed hard. After a few feet, the small channel broadened into a vast pool.

He took hold of the paddle and advanced with quick strokes. The surfboard glided through clumps of water lilies. The huge mass of floating green leaves brushed against the bottom and sides of the board and slowed it down to a crawl.

All around him, the water was dark and murky—sinister. A slight panic always caught him when he had to pass over the water lilies. He was afraid the paddles would get ensnared in the underwater stems, then something would grab him, pull him under and drown him. Every time, he had to fight panic, paddle carefully and push his way through the quicksand of water lilies.

Suddenly, he heard a racket on his left and spun around. A gray shadow took off into the air. He gave a start and fought to keep his balance. With his heart rumbling in his throat, he looked up and saw a gray heron flap its wings forcefully, disappearing over a tree. He goggled at it, panting, adrenaline pumping through his limbs like searing fire. He wanted to get away from that trap as soon as possible before something else startled him and he actually fell into the water, drowning himself in panic. In a burst of energy, he paddled away.

He cleared a bend around another huge bush and the secret spot came into view in all its splendor. Before him spread a wide, placid inlet, guarded on its front by the long stretch of reeds he had passed on the way to the gate, and on its back by thick woods. In its center, a bit to the right, a small island emerged from the water, surmounted by two stocky trees. Clusters of water lilies sprinkled the surface near the shores, contending the space with large bushes that seemed to grow out of the water.

The silence in the inlet was eerie, muffled and filled with expectation, only occasionally broken by the rustle of a hidden bird or the plop of a fish breaking the surface to catch its prey. It was as if the whole place was holding its breath for something

extraordinary. It looked like the lair of a fabled monster...
magical and mysterious.

Every time he visited the secret spot, it always filled him with
a vague sense of threat. The overgrown water lilies made him
think of mermaids living in secret in this hidden spot. Today, he
wouldn't have minded seeing a pair of eyes stare at him from
under one of those leaves. He wouldn't have minded a mermaid,
merman, or a bunch of them attacking him and trying to drown
him because he had discovered them. He wouldn't have minded
them chasing him home and waging war against him. Today, he
wished evil merpeople existed, so he'd have better things to fight
than Ms. Ambrose and his stupid classmates.

He was suddenly overwhelmed by longing for Acorn. He
wished he could see this place. He would have loved the secret
spot, he thought—it could have become their secret spot. He
sighed. It wasn't right—things were not right without him.
Acorn was his best friend and he had hurt him.

He needed to apologize.

Yes, he decided, he needed to.

He slipped his left oar into the water and veered the surfboard around.

As he reached the summit of the hill, he caught his breath.
Stains of perspiration darkened his T-shirt on his heaving back
and under his armpits. He inhaled deeply, stepped toward the
downhill slope, in the direction of his house.

He had been thinking about how to make peace with Acorn
for the last hour, and was still mulling over it. How was he ever
going to pull that one off? Acorn was really mad and scared.
How was he even going to get close to him? And what was he
going to do after he apologized? Was he going to go back to
things as usual? How? He couldn't see how. It was either people
or Acorn, it seemed. Maybe he could pretend, he thought. He
could make it look like he didn't care about Acorn anymore, but

then he'd actually ride him and play with him in the back of the house—not in the open, though, that was too risky. Perhaps, he should do what his father said: start playing football or baseball —something popular that could make him look normal. That could work...

A pale ray of hope broke through the cloud of despair in his mind. He didn't feel comfortable at all with pretending and he didn't even know if he had the energy or the smarts to pull it off, but what choice did he have? It was either be yourself or be alone. It just felt so unfair, so stupid! But then again: did he want to be unhappy for the rest of his life? What point was there in fighting everybody around you, if you wanted them to be your friends?

Through the growing foliage, he caught sight of the familiar ochre mass that was his house. He quickened his descent and soon came into view of the school. Acorn was grazing in the paddock near the street—he looked pretty relaxed. Maybe he had calmed down, he thought, and forgotten about the incident. He hoped so—he didn't want a repetition of the scene at his box. He cleared the last stretch of the slope and advanced toward the edge of the woods. As he was about to emerge in the open, he spotted some boys on their bicycles. Instinctively, he slowed down to a halt and hid behind a tree.

The group of kids stopped in front of the paddock.

He peeked out from behind the trunk and squinted. He recognized the people on the bikes: it was the same gang that had attacked him, plus another boy. Luka was at the head of the pack as usual.

He wondered if they had come to chase him and beat him up again, then he recognized the boy in their midst: Dan Muld-bridge. What was Dan doing with them? Had he joined the gang? How could that be? He craned his neck to get a better view.

Simon shoved Dan and told him something. Jamie strained his ears, but at that distance he couldn't hear a word. Dan shook his head and said something. Simon punched him in the head. Dan staggered back and looked for a way out, but the other boys laughed and shoved him back.

Jamie watched the scene with a faint sense of detachment. If Dan hadn't betrayed him so treacherously, he could probably feel bad for him. He still didn't like watching him being bullied, but why would he risk his skin for somebody who would stab him in the back as soon as he turned around?

Luka picked up a stone and handed it to Dan. He hesitated. Luka shoved the stone in at his chest and made him grab it. He spun him around and gestured toward Acorn, who was grazing in the paddock, his back turned away from them.

An awful presentiment seized Jamie. His whole body contracted in a spasm as he resisted the urge to run toward Luka and Dan to stop them.

In the distance, Luka bellowed, "Do it!"

Dan jolted as if struck by lightning. He swung his arm back and flung the stone. A second later, the projectile hit Acorn square in the back. He bolted and kicked furiously.

The boys roared with laughter.

Bewildered, Acorn wheeled around and stared at the sneering gang. Before he could make out what was going on, Luka bent down and grabbed more stones.

Jamie jumped out of his hiding place—he wanted to shout to Acorn, to warn him, to tell him to run away, but instead he choked, afraid the boys would hear him. For a second, he had the impression that Acorn turned his way and looked him straight in the eyes, then a pelting rain descended on him.

In horror, Jamie watched him fleeing toward the fence of the paddock. He came in too fast and jumped short. His right hoof crashed against the top plank. A loud crash of splintering wood reached Jamie's ears. In the distance, he saw a puff of bay hair blow in the air around Acorn's right foreleg.

"Oh, please, no, no!" he cried in a choked whisper. Don't let him be hurt, please don't! He stared transfixed as Acorn's whole body twisted in midair and dove out of balance toward the ground. For a split second, it looked like he was going to crash face-first, but then he whipped his huge neck back and drove his hooves deep into the ground. Clumps of earth exploded all around him as he heaved himself up with a loud groan.

Jamie held his breath. Acorn stumbled upright, then he rushed into his box, out of sight.

Luka and his gang high-fived each other, howling in triumph. They exchanged congratulatory elbowing and slaps. Electrified by their impunity, they jumped onto their bikes and swooped away.

Jamie watched as Dan, left behind, started rocking back and forth on the spot, probably panicking at the idea of either being framed for what had happened or seeing the boys turn around and come back to beat him up. When he finally felt safe, he jerked into action. He seized his bike from the ground and rushed away at full speed.

Jamie watched him disappear around the bend. He hid back behind the tree and felt a tremor driving through his whole body. He looked at his hands—they were shaking. He felt a tide of self-loathing swallow him. He hadn't lifted a finger to defend Acorn and now his friend was hurt. "Coward," he hissed.

He slid down against the bark of the tree, clasping his arms around his knees. The image of Acorn's head turning toward him flashed before his eyes. He had seen him, he was sure. He had seen him standing there hiding while those thugs threw stones at him. He hated himself; he wanted to rip himself apart. He was a coward, a filthy coward. He had betrayed Acorn, truly betrayed him. There was no turning back now—no pretending anymore. Acorn wasn't going to let him close ever again—and he was right. It was over.

The crash of Acorn's hoof against the fence coursed through Jamie's brain. He might be hurt, a voice whispered coldly inside him. You can't just wash your hands of it after what you've done. Jamie stirred. No, he couldn't. He must know whether he was hurt. It was his fault—he needed to make sure Acorn was all right or tell somebody so that they could take care of him.

With a huge effort, he stood up and made his way toward the paddock. Immediately, he stopped. No, he couldn't go that way. He couldn't be seen by Acorn—he would probably panic and hurt himself even more. He needed to hide in order to check on him.

A bitter laugh escaped his lips. So, that was how things stood —how deep he had dug his own grave... Well done, loser, he spat at himself. He started shaking again. Calm down, he ordered himself angrily. It is all your fault, so deal with it. You should have thought about it before acting like a coward!

He gritted his teeth and swallowed. He must check on Acorn first, then he could have his well-deserved pity party.

He turned back and made his way sideways through the woods. He followed the trail to the asphalt road, then crossed it and entered the woods that flanked his house.

When he knew he was at the height of Acorn's box, he left the trail and cut through the vegetation. Slowly, minding every single step in order not to make any noise, he tiptoed to the edge of the wood. When the planks of the paddock came into view, he crouched down behind a bush and peeked through the foliage.

Some twenty yards ahead, he spotted the open door of Acorn's box. He squinted and looked inside. Through the thick wall of shadow, he made out the his dark shape. He was standing very still with his head turned away toward a corner. He couldn't see his face very well, but his stillness troubled him.

He pulled out his toy telescope and pointed it toward the box. He struggled with the scratched plastic lenses for a while until he was able to put Acorn's body somewhat in focus. Carefully, he tilted the telescope down toward his hooves. A patch of hair was missing from his right leg, and in its place, a scratch ran all the way down to his hoof. The cut wasn't deep and there was only a little bit of swelling around it. Moreover, Acorn was leaning without problems on his foot, which meant that nothing was broken.

Jamie sighed with relief. He took his eye off of the telescope and drew a big shuddering breath. A shoot of hope rose timidly inside him. Since the wound was not that bad, then Acorn could recover quickly and maybe he'd forget what happened altogether. Maybe he could even try and approach him now.

He turned back at the box. In the distance, he could see Acorn still standing in the same spot, motionless. The hope inside him flickered. He raised his telescope again and looked. Through the scratches of the lenses, he saw Acorn's face hovering a few inches from the wall before him. He seemed to be staring through it, his eyes glossy and lifeless. He looked shell-shocked.

Jamie felt a knot tighten around his throat—it was his fault, all his fault. He looked away and leaned back, barely able to breathe. Acorn wasn't OK at all—he was hurt, badly hurt. He couldn't go near him or he would panic for sure.

The small hope that was left inside him evaporated instantly and, in its place, the raw edge of despair cut through him like a knife.

It was all over.

17

SIMPLE MATH

J amie woke up with a start. A sudden sense of urgency overwhelmed him. He turned his head on the pillow, straining his ears. After a second, a booming sound traveled through the walls, echoing in the silent house like the rumble of thunder.

Boom... Boom... Boom!

Jamie turned around, fully awake. In the room next door, he heard his parents jump out of bed and dart down the stairs.

Another shuddering boom echoed through the walls, then came a distant crash.

Jamie sat up and listened. His parents wrenched the door open and ran out, then there was silence. He waited. Nothing. It was probably just Dillinger acting up, he thought, kicking the box as he sometimes did when he had been cooped up too long. The crashing though... He must have broken something. He should go check if they needed help. He should, but his body felt soggy, heavy, a sense of dread still hanging in his chest.

Come on, he ordered himself. It might be important. Even if he was still upset with his parents, he didn't want them to get hurt if, for example, Brunga had broken out of his stall. The thought of their bull running loose on the property and charging them finally jerked him into action. With a groan, he slid off the bed.

He put on a fleece sweater and climbed down the stairs. He picked up a pair of working leather gloves from the basket near the kitchen door—just in case—then walked out.

The morning air was cold and damp—it must have rained during the night. The sun had just risen and it cast long shadows around the garden. He shivered and slid into the stables.

The warmth inside was palpable. Accumulated and stored overnight, the heat of the horses' bodies had become almost solid, weaved and textured with the fragrance of hay, wood shavings and the scent of their skin. It was homey, cozy, comfortably pleasant.

He walked up to Dillinger's box, but found it intact. Perplexed, he looked at it twice, making sure he wasn't missing something, but no, the door of the box was not damaged. He leaned in to check for scratches on Dillinger's legs—they were fine. That crashing noise couldn't have come from him, then. Dillinger glowered at him as Milly stood up on her hind legs, eager to get out.

"Don't worry, Dill," he said distractedly. He turned around and noticed that the massive door of the stables was ajar. Maybe Brunga then, he thought. He started at a jog.

As he sneaked out, something out of the corner of his eye caught his attention. He stopped in his tracks and spun around. A cold chill tingled through his body as he saw what was left of the door of Acorn's box. The metal frame hung crooked from the stables' wall like the broken jaw of a boxer. Acorn's shoes had etched deep marks into the inner panel. The fury of his kicks had caved it in and snapped it off the soldering around the edges. On the other side of the door, he saw splinters of the exterior wood ribs jutting out like broken teeth. The metal bolts pointed inward, twisted out of shape, while the two sockets lay sprawled on the cement pavement a few feet away.

He had never seen anything like it. Acorn must have gone berserk to wreak such havoc. But why? He had never acted out before. What had gotten into him? It looked as if he had felt trapped and panicked. But again why? Acorn had always been fine in his box and knew he or Mom would come to let him out. So, w—

His train of thought faltered as a horrible hunch surfaced in his mind. Perhaps that was exactly the problem—Acorn knew he would open the door. He must have panicked because he thought the friend he once trusted was going to hurt him.

Jamie flushed, stung by guilt, transfixed by the destruction before him.

Jan suddenly walked out of the box.

Jamie gave a start.

Jan noticed him. He swore loudly and kicked the wrecked door. "Look at this mess! And I pay, I pay for your stupid horse!" He kicked the broken door again, then stormed off.

Jamie stood nailed to the spot. At least it had been quick, he thought.

Maddie appeared around the corned. She glanced at Jan sulking back home, then noticed Jamie. Her expression sagged, then she composed herself and walked up to the box.

Jamie watched her in silence.

"What a mess..." she muttered, surveying the scene. "Did you guys fight or something?"

"No," he lied flatly.

Maddie turned around, narrowing her eyes.

Jamie had the impression she knew he was lying, but she didn't press on.

She rubbed her forearm distractedly and looked back at the box.

He noticed a slightly hysterical gleam in her eyes—she looked shaken.

"I just don't understand what got into him," she said hoarsely.

He did—at least he thought he did—but he shrugged, feigning ignorance.

"He didn't even touch his food. I gave a look inside and all the hay was still there—the oats too. I hope he's not ill or something."

Jamie frowned—Acorn hadn't touched his food? His stomach clutched in a tight knot. If he hadn't shouted at him, if he had defended him... With a mighty effort, he tore himself away from his guilty thoughts and asked the only question that really mattered, "Is he all right?"

"I think so. He scratched his right foreleg—he must have jumped the fence again. I knew he'd hurt himself one of these days. But apart from that, he's fine as far as I can tell. He wouldn't let me near him."

A wave of relief ran through Jamie. "Where is he?"

"He's down in the school," Maddie pointed in the distance. The sleeve of her shirt slid back, revealing a nasty, fresh bite mark on her forearm.

Jamie gasped. "He bit you!?"

She hastily pulled the shirt back over her arm. "It's all right, it's not too bad. I just don't understand what got into him. I didn't do anything to freak him out. I just bent down to see how his leg was."

Jamie blanched. Oh, he knew too well why Acorn bit Mom: he thought she was picking up stones to throw at him!

"Kitten, are you all right?"

Jamie sucked in a painful breath and composed himself. "Yeah. I just can't believe he bit you." Lies, he thought. What he really couldn't believe was how easy and automatic lying was becoming. A lurch of disgust for his own treachery hit his stomach.

"Anyway," Maddie said, "we can't do anything right now. You need to go to school. We'll just let him cool off and we'll see about him later." She steered him around and led him back toward the stables. "Come on, I'll fix you some breakfast."

He shook his head. "No, thanks. I'm not hungry." He felt noxious in fact. "I'll just eat some bread."

"Come on, kitten, you can't start the morning on an empty stomach."

"No, really, I woke up too fast." Lies again, he thought. "The racket Acorn made. My stomach is all up in a twist." Lies, lies, lies.

"OK... I'll pack you something for later, then."

"Thanks." He threw one last glance at the wrecked door and then beyond, toward the school where Acorn had fled. He suddenly wondered whether he would ever see him again.

As soon as they got back into the house, he walked upstairs and took his time getting changed into his working clothes. He wanted to spend as little time as possible under the scrutiny of his mom. He couldn't bear the idea of having to tell her about what had really happened.

He took care of his morning chores as quickly as he could, then took a shower, and walked down into the kitchen to pack his lunch.

Maddie finished wrapping two sandwiches and a couple of apples.

He stuffed everything inside his backpack and kissed her good-bye. "See you later," he said, but he actually wished she had enough to do that he could avoid her.

"OK," Maddie replied listlessly.

He was taken aback by the tone of her voice, but didn't say anything. He turned around and went to get his bike.

As he pedaled alongside the hedge, he cast a glance at the school.

Acorn looked back at him, wary and tense.

He wrenched his eyes away and tried to focus on the road. He still couldn't believe Acorn had bitten his mom. He wouldn't have been surprised if he had chewed his head off or kicked him, but Mom... He must really be shocked beyond measure to do something like that.

Yeah, he scoffed to himself, what do you expect? The image of the destruction Acorn had visited upon his box flashed again in front of his eyes. His stomach plunged. The truth was that he didn't want to believe Acorn could be so hurt. He didn't want to accept the responsibility of what he had done. Things were bad enough already.

A wave of loneliness and self-pity washed over him. He snorted. Right, he thought scornfully, you could feel pity for yourself if it weren't all your fault, but it is. You should never have treated Acorn as you did.

He gritted his teeth. If only he could desert himself and be someone else, abandon his life and take that of someone else. A sense of claustrophobia pressed on him. He felt incurably stuck, imprisoned in his own body, alone.

The school loomed into view. He blinked and came back to his senses—he had completely lost track of time. Back into the cage, he thought gloomily.

He rode his bike to the back of the building and locked it next to the ones of his classmates. He composed himself, ordering himself to be alert and careful, then opened the big metal-and-glass back door and stepped inside.

As he was about to reach his classroom, a man and a woman he had never seen walked in from the front door. They both wore dark suits and were carrying briefcases that looked very official. He sized them up and wondered whether they were someone's parents. Where was their kid, though? Maybe they were new teachers, then.

The two looked around, then headed toward Mr. Culvert's office.

New teachers, Jamie decided. They looked as mean as Ms. Ambrose. Not much was going to change there.

He trudged into his classroom and sat down next to Sara. She pretended he didn't exist as she had done successfully for the past week.

He couldn't stop thinking about Acorn. What happened was all his fault and he didn't know what to do about it. He heard brisk steps approach through the door and rose to his feet automatically. He was about to say the usual "Good morning, Ms. Ambrose," when he saw Mr. Culvert walking in.

The principal gestured the class to sit down and said, "Ms. Ambrose will be a few minutes late. You will all remain seated while you wait for her." He then turned around and walked out, closing the door behind him.

Did he actually think anybody would listen? Jamie turned around and in fact half the class was already on their feet.

Luka and Simon threw the glass door at the back of the room open and ran onto the basketball court. Alex, George, and Daniel Maltby followed suit.

Jamie stood up and trailed the line of people trickling out into the open air. A few feet in front of him, Holly and Francesca were chatting and gesticulating over a girl magazine. Right behind them, Dan was deep in a whispered conversation with Elizabeth.

Jamie felt a sudden surge of anger. He strode up to Dan. "You and Luka are getting closer these days, uh!?"

Dan blinked, dumbfounded. "What...?"

Jamie sneered. "Playing skipping stones, Dan?"

He blanched, his eyes widening in terror.

Jamie felt the urge to punch him—he wanted to, but instead he spun around and walked away. He thought saying these things would made him feel better. It didn't—it made him feel worse. He was taking it out on the weak ones now. He was turning into a bully, just like Luka. If he was so angry, why didn't he stand up to him, instead of threatening Dan? Was he afraid of Luka? No, he told himself resolutely. Not of Luka. He just didn't want to feel lonely. He didn't want to feel lonely anymore!

He leaned against the wall and watched with starving eyes his classmates playing happily. Luka stole the ball from Alex's hands and went for a two-pointer. The basketball flew in a nice arc and dove through the hoop with a satisfying whoosh. Simon cheered. For a split second, the image of Luka throwing stones at Acorn flashed in front of Jamie's eyes.

"Hi!"

Jamie startled. He spun around and found Sara standing next to him. She flicked a quick smile in his direction and waited.

"Hi," he grumbled. What did she want? She had pretended he didn't exist for a whole week and now she just sneaked up on him? He waited for her to say something and when she didn't, he turned around and resumed watching the game.

"You're not crazy, Jamie," Sara said all of a sudden.

He turned around.

They looked at each other for a second, then Sara lowered her eyes. "And I did see Ms. Ambrose slap Dan."

Jamie blinked. "So why didn't you say that instead of calling me crazy?"

"I didn't call you crazy."

He wanted to retort something, but then he remember she was right. It was Dan who had called him crazy, not her. Everything was getting muddled in his head. He shrugged and turned around.

Sara swallowed. She seemed to struggle with herself.

Jamie took in what she had just said: she had lied. He looked at his classmates laughing and having fun—they too had lied. All the rage, the spite, the betrayal he had felt at the way he had been treated, crashed back against him like a tidal wave. How could they walk around perfectly happy and smiling after having hurt him like that? How could they even look at themselves in the mirror?

"My mom..." Sara struggled.

Jamie turned back.

"My mom told me that if somebody asked, I should say that Ms. Ambrose didn't do anything."

Jamie smiled bitterly—of course she did. She was the class rep after all, the same awful woman who had defended Ms. Ambrose when his mom had gone to talk to her. Nice family they were. "Great, so what?"

Sara flushed violently. "I-I just thought you had the right to know."

"The right to know? Why don't you go and tell them!" He gestured toward his classmates.

She threw a fearful glance around but didn't move.

"Well, thanks a lot, Sara! Thanks for lying, for letting everybody tear me to pieces. Thanks for not talking to me for a whole week. Thanks for nothing!"

Her delicate eyelashes fluttered in shock. She spun around and scurried away.

Jamie's blood started buzzing as if a swarm of bees needed a way out. He trusted Sara—she was the smartest in their class, his desk mate—and she had betrayed him, had not spoken out, had lied, had let everybody taunt him and bully him. She deserved his spite, she deserved it! Yet, he felt like a total jerk for lashing out at her. She was the only one who had come forward and talked to him, who had admitted she had lied—and he had just bitten her like a rabid dog!

Something inside him stirred, reaching out beyond his skin. This whole thing—whatever it was—had to stop. He wanted his life back, all of his life back now. A scorching thirst clutched at his throat. He passed his tongue over his lips and turned toward Luka, Alex and the other boys playing in the court. He knew how to play. He was like them—he could show them. With a good play he could erase the stain of what had happened. He could redeem himself. Even Luka would have to admit he was good and even if he didn't, somebody else would. Then everything would go back to normal. This thing had to stop, it had to stop.

He noticed that the team Alex was leading had only three players—him, Daniel and George—against the four of Luka's. That was his chance. He kicked away from the wall and headed feverishly to the court. Suddenly, he stopped. What if Luka didn't let him play with the other boys? No, Luka didn't know he had seen him throw stones at Acorn. He was fine. Maybe he would call him Horseboy, but that was it. He just needed to show him he could play and he wouldn't beat him up in front of everybody. Plus, he wasn't going to play in his team. It was up to Alex to let him play—he could convince him.

"Can I play with you?" he blurted out and, without waiting for an answer, wedged himself in. "You're one man down. I'll play with you!"

Alex pretended he didn't hear and passed the ball to George.

Jamie barely registered Alex's reaction. He wasn't going to let his chance slip. Alex didn't say no, so he was going to take it as an implicit yes and play. He zeroed in on the game, sprinted forward and, on a long rebound, he caught the ball.

"Give it back!" Luka bellowed almost instantly.

Jamie didn't hear him. All he could think about was that he

had the ball—he had his chance. As he raised his eyes, he saw Luka reach forward. He sprang into action and dribbled the basketball away from his hand, jumping out of reach.

Luka missed and stumbled. He straightened up, his ears red-hot with fury and embarrassment. "Watcha think you're doing, clown!?"

Jamie turned, ready to make a grand pass, but Alex, George and Daniel all looked indecisive. Well then, he was going to score himself, he thought. He was going to make it work anyway, one way or the other. He turned back just in time to catch sight of Luka rushing against him.

He whipped back, made a quick feint and dribbled, passing on his right. It wasn't that different than playing with Acorn, he thought. Suddenly, Luka's elbow flashed in his field of view— pain exploded in his mouth. He stumbled. Through the haze, he made out Luka reaching again for the ball. No way!

He bounced the ball away from his outstretched hand and went for the hoop. Suddenly, he felt his right foot being hooked. He tripped and fell to the ground. His hands went hot as loose gravel from the asphalt pavement growled under his weight. It was a fault, but he wasn't going to call it. If he did, they'd call him a wuss and not let him play with them, he knew it. He looked up: the ball was going to bounce out of bounds.

He scrambled up—he could still make it! He rushed forward, seized the ball at the line and spun around.

Luka growled as he skid to a halt in front of him, but he jumped and threw.

Luka shoved him back in midair.

He caught sight of the ball diving into the hoop for a clean two-pointer, then he felt his back clatter and his teeth click into his skull as he hit the ground. His hands went hotter than before, but he didn't care. He had made it!

He jumped up and ran to his teammates, raising his hand in

a high five. "So, what's the score?" he yapped happily. Alex, Daniel and George didn't answer. Instead, they goggled at him with a mix of repulsion and incredulity.

"You dumb-ass, look what you've done!" Luka barked.

Jamie turned around and saw him holding the basketball with the tip of his fingers, disgusted at the sight of a spot of blood on it.

He frowned and looked down at his hands: blood was oozing out of a series of deep scratches filled with gravel. He blanched. No, no, no! "I'm sorry, I'll clean it!" he said, hastily rubbing his hands on his shirt.

A fit of hysterical laughter burst around him.

Luka flung the ball at him and walked away. "Game's over, weirdo!"

The ball bounced off his chest and rolled away. He watched the smear of blood flash around like the red symbol of a slot machine, picking up asphalt gravel as it went. He had lost his hand. He turned and faced his other classmates. Alex, Daniel and George were still goggling at him as if he had just landed from another planet. Alex shook his head contemptuously, then they all walked away.

Jamie caught sight of his reflection in the open glass door of his classroom and a hot surge of shame prickled through his skin—he looked like a train wreck. Blood oozed out of deep scratches in his knees and hands; smears of blood soiled his T-shirt; and more blood trickled on his chin from a deep cut in his swollen lower lip.

He flushed—now he understood the look of repulsion in his classmates' eyes. Had he lost his mind? What was he thinking? Was he even thinking at all? How could he go overboard like that without even realizing it?

As the pain in his body became real, he noticed that the rest of his classmates were staring at him and whispering. Not again, he thought desperately, not again... But he had done it again. He had made a show of himself. He had made a fool of himself!

Sara stared horrified.

Jamie bent his head down and doggedly headed for the side door. He was going to the nurse to get fixed up. He didn't want anybody else to see him like that, especially not Ms. Ambrose or Mr. Culvert. He walked up to the door and stopped. His eyes flicked between his bloodied hands and the doorknob, his brain jammed and dizzy. He didn't want to smear the doorknob—he didn't want to leave traces. Out of the daze, he heard running footsteps approaching.

"Here!" Sara called out, handing him her handkerchief.

He stared at it blankly.

"Take it," she urged. "You can keep it. I don't need it."

OK, he thought, exhausted. He picked up the handkerchief. "Thanks," he muttered without looking at Sara.

He wrapped the fabric around the doorknob and pulled the door open.

As he entered the corridor, he saw Alan come to a stop at the bottom of the stairs and turn toward him. He looked shocked.

"Are you all right?" Alan asked out of breath.

He nodded with clenched jaws.

Alan hesitated, then said in a pleading whisper, "I didn't think they could bully you..."

"Yeah, well..." Jamie felt a weight drop inside his stomach and drag him down. So, he had let Alan down. On top of everything, he had let down someone who looked up to him. Great. He walked away without looking at him.

"I...," Alan trailed off behind him. "I should have helped you!"

Jamie stopped in his tracks. What...?

"It was my turn." Alan said in a hoarse voice.

Jamie suddenly remembered what they had told each other

when they had shaken hands: next time, you'll help me out. He turned around.

Alan stared at him, dripping with shame, then he spun around and rushed up the stairs.

Jamie followed him with his eyes. A wave of gratitude toward this kid he barely knew surged inside him. It wasn't your fault, Alan, he thought. It was my fault. I made this mess.

Drained, he turned around and trudged toward the infirmary. As he cleared the corner, Ms. Ambrose suddenly appeared in front of him. Jamie froze. Like a bloodhound smelling wounded prey, she had found him.

Startled by his appearance, Ms. Ambrose froze too. She looked livid and for a second he thought she was going to kick him, instead a gloating sneer started stretching across her bony face.

He looked away—he couldn't stand the nasty satisfaction she was getting at seeing him hurt.

The sneer didn't last long though and it was soon replaced by a worried furrow. "You better not blame this mess on me, boy," she said. "I didn't have anything to do with it. I wasn't even near you. I have witnesses."

He frowned. What was she worried about? That he would go home and tell mommy? We had all seen how well that had worked out.

A flash suddenly passed over Ms. Ambrose's features as if she had caught herself saying too much. "Go to Ms. Haley and clean yourself up."

He didn't need to be told twice. He slinked away immediately, thankful to escape her toxic presence.

He crept down the corridor to the nurse's office, holding his hands high, trying not to drip any blood on the floor.

What Ms. Ambrose had just said played back in his mind. A low growl escaped his lips. She had been better off keeping her mouth shut. He had forgotten about it, but now he remembered too well: she had everything to do with it: she had started it all. How could have he forgotten, he wondered. How could something like that escape his mind? Was he stupid or what?

He reached the nurse's office and found Ms. Haley gossiping on the phone.

At the sight of his bleeding scratches, she tilted her pretty head and snorted impatiently. "Sorry, I've got to go," she said to the person on the other end of the line. She snapped the phone shut and gestured him to sit down.

Jamie was always amazed by how her manners differed so much from her looks. Ms. Haley was a light-framed, pretty blonde in her early thirties. The first time he had met her, in second grade, he had expected her to be nice, since she was such a delicate-looking person and a nurse, but instead she had been rough and impatient from the start.

She flipped his hands unceremoniously and examined his bleeding scratches. "Why do you boys always have to fight like animals?"

Her hate stung. "I didn't fight," he said stiffly.

"Yes you did! Why do you boys always have to lie?"

"Why are you a nurse if you hate us so much!?"

Ms. Haley recoiled. Her face contorted as if she had been caught red-handed at a murder scene, then the luster of her beauty glossed it all over again. "I don't hate anybody," she said mechanically.

Yes you do, Jamie snarled in his mind. Why on Earth was he still wasting his time with these people!?

He stopped dead, struck by the thought. Yes, why?

"Here, let me see this," Ms. Haley said in a honeyed tone. She picked up his hand and started cleaning his wounds dotingly.

Jamie looked away—she was not a good actress. She hated her job, she probably hated all the boys in the school, but she pretended she cared. Such a life seemed like a terrible punishment to live. He didn't want to grow up like that. Then why was he too trying so hard to make all the nasty people around him like him? He didn't want to be friends with them—he didn't want to have anything to do with them. Then why? Because they were people and not a horse and he was supposed to be one of them? They weren't worth the dirt under Acorn's hooves. They were awful! He was far better off with Acorn.

He paused. He was, but Acorn was gone. They had wrenched him away from him. He stopped again. No, he told himself, you pushed him away. They just bullied you, but it was you who shoved Acorn away, you who flung the ball at him, you who didn't defend him when Luka and the other punks attacked him. You betrayed him, not anybody else.

A hot surge of self-hatred filled his chest. And you were a fool, he continued. You made the biggest mistake of your life, and all because you were so afraid of being alone. But you see, you've never been alone—you had the best friend in the whole wide world and you betrayed him... Just like that.

Jamie swallowed the bitter truth and took it in.

"There you go," Ms. Haley said cheerfully. "Like new."

He looked down at the band-aids on his hands and stood up. "Thank you," he said automatically and walked out of the infirmary.

"You're welcome!" he heard Ms. Haley chirp behind him. What a fake, he thought, and slowly made his way back to the classroom.

A thought jumped back in his mind. When he had walked to the court to play, he had actually worried that if the others knew what Luka had done, then he might feel embarrassed and not let him play. He snorted. How on Earth did he get to think like that? Instead of wanting to bash Luka's head in because he had hurt his best friend, he had worried he might not accept him? He had wanted the approval of a thug who had hurt his best friend. He had actually longed for it. How messed up was that? It was crazy! And that wasn't all. Then, he had even tried to win him over. He hadn't just betrayed Acorn with his actions and thoughts, but he had betrayed himself, who he was, what he believed in.

So, this was the life ahead of him if he chose it: lie, hide himself, betray everyone and everything he believed in.

"No way!" His voice echoed loud and clear against the walls.

No way! He refused to live like that. If he had to be alone from now on, then so be it. At least he was going to be himself. He liked who he was and hated who he had become—what they had bullied him into becoming. He was not going forward on this road and to hell with them.

A sudden sense of deep power surged through him. To hell with them, he repeated in his mind.

He took a deep breath and knocked at the door of his classroom.

"Come in," Ms. Ambrose called from behind the opaque glass.

He walked in. Immediately, he felt the eyes of his classmates turn. Let them think what they want, he thought, and sat down at his desk. He felt the skin on his back prickle, sure that they were pinning all sorts of judgments on him. Let them. He knew who he was now. They could think whatever they pleased.

There was only one thing he wanted to get straight with them.

"Go on," Ms. Ambrose told Holly, who was standing at the blackboard next to an unsolved equation.

Holly turned and resumed solving the problem. She furrowed her forehead in concentration, mumbled something under her breath, then scribbled the result of her calculations in white chalk.

"Good," Ms. Ambrose said flatly.

Holly hesitated, confused by the tone of her voice.

Ms. Ambrose raised her brow. "You may go back to your seat now."

Holly dropped the chalk in the holder and scuttled back to her desk.

Ms. Ambrose turned to the class. "Who wants to solve the next equation?"

Jamie raised his hand.

She blinked, then looked around for someone else, but the rest of the class was ducking away. She turned back and eyed him suspiciously.

He looked back blankly.

"Very well." She gestured him to stand up.

Jamie walked to the blackboard. He had no idea what he was doing. He erased the previous equation and waited.

Ms. Ambrose started dictating, "If two epsilon plus seven..."

Jamie turned and started writing:

$2y+7=$

Then inspiration struck. He leaned in closer to the board and scribbled feverishly:

$2y+7=$ I LOVE ACORN!!!!

The classroom exploded with laughter.

Ms. Ambrose turned bright red with fury and shouted, "Erase that!"

Jamie wheeled around, the chalk clutched in his hand like a sword. "No!" he yelled back, "I don't care what you say. You're wrong!" Then he turned to face the class. "All of you!"

Some of his classmates flinched, stunned, but Luka and a group of others howled and jeered back.

"I like Acorn too!" Sara called out suddenly.

Jamie turned, taken aback.

She glanced back at him, blushing violently.

"'Cause you're a weirdo too," Luka called, "Horsegirl!"

"Hey!" shouted Jamie, rounding on him. He threw back his arm and flung the chalk. The projectile hit Luka square in the forehead and exploded in a puff of white dust.

Luka flinched and toppled over, crashing onto the ground with a loud bang.

The room boomed with more laughter.

"That's for Acorn," Jamie said aloud.

"What do you think you're doing!?" barked Ms. Ambrose. She clawed at his arm and wrenched him around. Her face blue with rage, she raised her right hand high.

The air was suddenly sucked out of the classroom as everybody held their breath.

Jamie yanked his arm free and glowered defiantly at her. Come on, hit me, he thought wildly. Hit me and I'll hit you back!

But Ms. Ambrose hesitated. She glanced at the door, then back at Jamie, her pupils gaping wide as if she couldn't focus.

She's afraid to hit me, Jamie realized. She's afraid! An exultant grin flashed on his face.

Ms. Ambrose caught his insolent smile. Her face turned a sickly shade of green and started shaking convulsively. "Erase that," she croaked with repressed fury.

As an answer, he stepped back and dropped the eraser into the holder, then he turned around and walked back to his seat.

Ms. Ambrose stood rooted to the spot, transfixed.

Jamie sat down at his desk, his ears red hot as his resolution. He looked back.

Ms. Ambrose gave a start, seized the eraser and started dabbing violently at the blackboard.

Jamie felt a nudge on his arm and turned. Sara flashed a daring grin at him. He grinned back. He had not expected she would stick her neck out like that and felt a wave of admiration filling him with warmth. He had misjudged her and was glad she had proven him wrong.

He turned and studied his classmates. Holly was looking at him with a pained smile. A strange smile that filled him with sadness. He wished they could both go back to that beautiful day in March when she had stepped up bravely to meet Acorn and they had become friends, but she looked so different now, so far away from that girl. Behind her, Dan was goggling at him, thunderstruck. Something kept shifting feverishly in his eyes. Jamie wished he could understand him, he wished he could trust him again.

He turned back and watched Ms. Ambrose wipe off the chalk letters from the dark surface of the blackboard. It didn't matter, he thought. She might erase the words, but the message won't go away.

He could feel the eyes of his classmates on him again. Now you know, he thought—I'm not hiding anymore.

18

CATCHING A HORSE BY THE TAIL

J amie pushed hard on the pedals. The air whistled in his ears as he clipped forward at full speed. He felt alive again. The sun shone warm on his skin and a wild hope took hold of him. After setting the score straight with his classmates and Ms. Ambrose, he felt he could do anything.

Even get Acorn back.

He didn't want to give up on him. If there was the remotest possibility of getting his best friend back, he must try. He had done anything he could to push him away, so he must do as much and more to get him back.

How he'd manage that, he still didn't know. A knot tightened in his stomach and his hope floundered. He knew that once the trust of a horse for his rider was broken, there was no turning back. There must be exceptions, though, he thought desperately. He and Acorn were different: they had known each other since they were very little. They were basically brothers. That must mean something... Actually, it probably just made things worse. Their bond was special and he had torn it apart with his own hands. He had betrayed everything they were and for that Acorn must hate him furiously. Nevertheless he must try. He didn't want to give up.

He skidded to a halt in front of the iron gate of his house and pulled it open. He dropped his bike in the garden and ran up to the wicket gate that led toward the paddocks. As he passed through, he spotted his mom staring with a worried frown into the school.

She turned around and gasped. "Oh my God, what happened to you!?"

Jamie stopped in his tracks—he had completely forgotten. He glanced at his band-aided palms and instinctively passed his tongue over his swollen lip. "Nothing. I just fell playing basketball. It's my fault really—I was being stupid—not that Luka didn't help, though."

"That Luka again!? I'm gonna go talk to the parents of that little thug once and for all."

Jamie shook his head, "No, it's all right, Mom. I can handle it."

She raised her brows, taken aback by the tone of self-assurance in his voice.

He was surprised too. Yes, he thought, he could handle Luka. No matter what he did, he was not going to let him bully him anymore.

"Are you sure?"

He nodded. "I got it."

"OK... But you'll tell me if anything is wrong, right?"

"Yes."

Maddie nodded and her expression darkened. She turned and stared grimly toward the school. "I think we have a problem."

Jamie followed her gaze and caught sight of Acorn glowering back at them, tense and alert.

"He still won't let me near him. I get some ten feet from him, then he bolts away, snapping and kicking. I—"

"It's my fault."

She turned back. "What do you mean?"

Time to tell the truth, Jamie thought. Time to go back to the old ways. He looked up and drew a big breath. "I threw a basketball at him. I scared him. He got mad. Then Luka and his gang threw stones at him. I didn't defend him. I think he's right being mad at people, especially at me."

"It's my fault too."

Jamie fell silent, startled by the sorrow in his mom's voice.

She looked at him in the eyes. "You were already under enough stress. I shouldn't have dragged you to Ms. Ambrose looking like that and I should have smacked your father in the face for saying those awful things about you. I'm sorry."

"It's OK," he mumbled awkwardly.

"No, it's not OK." Maddie shook her head. "I should have talked to you, but I thought you hated me after what I did."

"I don't hate you, Mom." He had been mad at her, that was true, but he never hated her.

She hugged him tight. "Thank you, baby."

He hugged her back and felt a huge weight slide off his chest —Mom had apologized. She knew she had hurt him and she was sorry. That was enough for him. He had his mom back, now he needed to get his best friend back. That might be a bit more difficult, if not straight out impossible, but he had to try—it was his time to apologize.

Maddie seemed to read his mind. She pulled back and turned toward Acorn. "We're gonna fix this. I'm gonna go talk to Dr. Malkin. I'll get him to give us some tranquilizer and we'll take it from there."

Jamie winced. "Do you want to knock Acorn out?"

"No, just enough to make him manageable. I'll borrow Dr. Malkin's tranquilizing gun."

"You wanna shoot him!!!?"

Maddie hunched her shoulders. "It's just easier, Jamie. He's not gonna feel anything—just a prick."

"I don't want to shoot him. He's not crazy!"

"Nobody's saying he is crazy, dear. It's just easier that way. He won't let us near him otherwise."

"Can't we do it another way?"

She sighed. "I don't think so. I need him out of the school by the evening. There are some classes and your father is away. I need to teach them and I still have to go buy some groceries." She checked her watch and frowned. "Which means I've got to go out now or I won't make it." She turned Jamie and led him away from the fence. "There is some chicken in the oven and some zucchini on the stove. You think you can manage?"

He nodded.

"And if you have time, throw in some hay to the sheep, please. I forgot to."

"OK."

"I'll be back in an hour, then we'll take care of Acorn together." Jamie nodded.

"I'm sure you two will make peace again. You just need some time."

He peeked up and saw a shade of doubt in her eyes. She too knew that the chances were slim.

She gave him a peck on the cheek and she was off.

Jamie waited until the sound of the car faded away, then he pulled out the chicken from the oven. He stared blankly at it, lost in thought. He didn't like the idea of shooting tranquilizer into Acorn. He had seen it done to an elephant in a documentary on TV once and the memory still made him uneasy. It seemed so disrespectful. He understood it might be necessary, but he still didn't want to do it. There was also something else: he didn't want anybody else to take care of Acorn. It was their problem, their friendship, and they needed to sort it out in their own way. If there was still a way of patching things up, of course.

He sighed. Time was running out. Soon it would be too late to make peace with him. He still didn't have a plan, but he also didn't have any more time. It was now or never! He'd have to improvise.

"Fine," he said testily to the empty kitchen. He walked up to the door and grabbed a pair of leather gloves. He had half an idea—it wasn't a plan, just a hunch, the first thing his brain had thrown at him, but it was better than nothing and as good as anything else at this point.

He ran out and rushed to the tack room. He grabbed a longe and quickly fastened a slipknot on one end. Then he darted out of the clubhouse and into the stables. He dropped a measure of oats into a plastic bucket, put the longe around his shoulder and opened Dillinger's box. He pulled out Milly and led her out.

As they approached the wooden gate of the school, he spotted Acorn in the far corner on the other side, near the road. He drew the bolt out, led Milly in, then locked the gate behind him. He took a deep breath and started walking toward him.

As he saw him approaching, Acorn raised his head and studied him, on his guard. He was probably wondering what he was doing with Milly on one side and a bucket of oats on the other.

When Jamie got about fifteen feet away from Acorn, he stopped. "It's all right," he said soothingly. Careful not to make any sudden movements, he bent down and released Milly.

She darted forward and skidded to a halt in front of Acorn, bleating for attention.

He lowered his head and nudged her affectionately.

The diversion had worked. Jamie sprang into action. In one fluid motion, he grabbed the head of the longe, threw his arm back and flung the makeshift lasso high in the air.

Acorn gave a start and jerked his head up as the noose descended on him with a whisper. The knot fastened tightly around his neck. As soon as he felt the yoke tying him down, Acorn shied violently.

Milly shot away, bleating in panic.

Jamie twisted the longe in a snare around his right hand and tugged back, but the might of Acorn's pull jolted him off his feet. He flew into the air and landed face down in the sand.

Acorn bolted toward the fence.

Jamie scrambled up, but a second huge tug jerked him forward. He stumbled, trying to keep on his feet.

Acorn jumped.

Jamie tugged back desperately.

Acorn groaned angrily and smashed through the top plank of the fence. He careened on the other side, whipped himself back on balance and lunged forward again.

Jamie felt the longe drive him against the fence. He tried desperately to untie the snare around his wrist, but found he couldn't. "No, no, no!" he screamed in panic, then jumped blindly. With a loud crack he crashed against the middle plank. A shock of pain stabbed his legs as if somebody had clubbed him in the thighs. Splinters went flying everywhere around him, then the ground drove against his shoulder with a grinding crunch.

He tumbled on the grass on the other side of the fence, grunting in pain. A split second later, his whole body was dragged at full speed across the asphalt and into the fields.

The ground rushed under him, tearing and biting at his clothes. In an instant, a storm of grass, dust and debris enveloped him. It felt like being scraped raw in a stone grinder.

It was hell! Now, wrapping the longe in a snare around his wrist seemed like the stupidest thing he could have ever done. He had expected Acorn would rear, kick, buckle and toss him around for half an hour or so, then get tired and see reason. But this!? This was madness! Acorn was going to kill him! He thought he should have listened to his mom, but it was too late to go back: if he let go, it was over—he wasn't going to get another chance. So he held onto the longe with both hands as if it was the last thing he was going to do on this Earth. He had to make this work.

"I'm not letting go, you hear me! I'm not letting you go!" he shouted at the top of his lungs. He twisted around, dug his heels into the ground and tugged hard.

Acorn stumbled. He slowed down for a couple of steps, then gave an angry jerk with his neck.

Jamie's knees buckled and a second later he was rolling and tumbling in the dust again. Now the tranquilizer gun seemed a perfectly legitimate way of dealing with Acorn! He would have shot him happily with his own hands if he could.

Acorn puffed forward like a locomotive. He cut through a field of wild daffodils, trailing him behind like a toy cart.

The stems of the flowers lashed at Jamie's face, blinding him. "I'll send you to the glue factory, you hear me!? I swear, I'm going to kill you when we stop!"

Acorn veered abruptly.

Jamie rolled around in a wide arc, then shot forward again. The crunching noise of grass rushing under his back turned into a sloshing sound. His body started dragging harder on the ground. They must have turned toward Turtle Pond, he thought. Not smart, buddy, not smart! He wriggled around to gloat at Acorn's struggle. The grin on his face collapsed as he spotted turtle shells hurtling toward him. "You've got to be kidding me!" he hissed under his breath.

Like a worm on an electric wire, he twisted out of the way as the hard shells grazed by and whizzed at his sides. "Enough!" he bellowed. He better stop this madness before he was knocked unconscious. He squirmed around and planted his feet, pulling with his whole body. A wave of mud lifted around his legs.

Acorn groaned like a breaking pulley.

"Stop, you stubborn mule, stop!"

Acorn snorted angrily and plowed on.

Jamie slipped in the mud and his head smacked hard against the shell of a turtle. A sea of stars exploded in front of his eyes. Blinded by pain, he struggled to keep hold of the longe. He turned on his back, dimly aware of being dragged again. His head felt as if it had been split open. His eyes streaming with tears, he blinked, trying to regain his bearings. Suddenly, he heard Acorn's hooves splash into water. He wheeled around just in time to see him plunge into Turtle Pond.

He drew a sharp intake of breath, then the pond swallowed him. The gelid water slapped him awake. He spun around, made out top from bottom and kicked for the surface.

He broke out of the water on Acorn's side, sputtering and floundering to keep afloat. "You crazy, proud horse! You wanna kill me or something!?"

Acorn shot him a scorching glance, apparently exasperated to find him still trailing him, then swam on, puffing like a steamboat. Turtles ducked away as he cut through the whole length of the pond.

Jamie saw him aim toward the opposite shore. He spotted the red bark of oak trees near the water. An idea struck.

He got hold of the longe with his left hand and, helping himself with his teeth, he unfastened the snare around his right. As the blood flowed back, he yelped in pain. His right hand felt as if it had been mauled. Grimacing, he closed and opened his fingers until some feeling came back to them. He tried to grasp the longe with his right again, but his hand was too swollen and weak. Since that didn't work, he brought his right arm forward, coiled the longe around it, then levered against it and pulled himself forward with his left, kicking with his feet. That way, he slowly climbed toward Acorn.

When he thought he had enough of the longe behind him, he stopped. Carefully, he started retrieving the rope and feeding it into a nice loose coil.

The shore was getting closer.

Jamie held on, catching his breath. He could hear Acorn's labored breathing now—finally he was wearing out.

They reached shallow water and started climbing out.

As soon as his feet touched the bottom, Jamie sprinted forward at full speed.

Acorn glanced at him blankly, too spent to focus on anything else other than catching his breath.

Jamie shot toward the closest oak tree. He threw the longe a couple of times around the trunk, fed the head through a coil, then clumsily tightened a rudimentary knot with his numb hands.

Acorn made to walk away, but the longe snapped tight and tugged him back. He stumbled and twisted around. Spotting the yoke, he gave a pull and realized he was stuck. Gasping for air, he glowered at Jamie.

He glared back grimly, his clothes torn and ripped, his face and arms covered in scratches.

They stared at each other for a minute, full of contempt for each other's stubbornness.

"You feel better now?" Jamie said at last, drawing himself up with a groan. "Are we even?"

Big clouds of steam whipped away from Acorn's skin, enshrouding him in a hellish glow, at the center of which his furious eyes glowered at him unflinchingly, accusingly. No, they were not even.

Jamie's heart sank. "Yeah, I know," he said roughly. "I screwed up. I screwed up bad, Acorn, but I'm sorry. I really am, OK? I came here to apologize if you just let me." It wasn't much of an apology, he knew, but he couldn't bring himself to feel too contrite after being dragged for half an hour through grit and mud and almost drowned.

His eyes fell on his swollen right hand. It still hurt like a bite from hell. He didn't mind the physical pain so much, though. At least the scratches and swelling he could see. He could cure them and eventually he would see them go away. Not like the pain inside his and Acorn's hearts. That he couldn't see and didn't know how to heal. He sighed. He must try, though, and he better be convincing at it if he really wanted Acorn back.

He looked up and inhaled deeply, forcing himself to forget about the pain in his body and the outrage of being dragged around like a puppet. Only his friend was important now—he owed it to him. He gathered his courage and walked carefully toward him.

As he saw him approach, Acorn flared his nostrils and drew back.

Jamie stopped in his tracks. A terrible sense of loss flooded him as he watched his old friend seized by fear before him. "It's me, Acorn. It's me. Please…"

Acorn's ears twitched. He stopped tugging and stood still.

A desperate hope got hold of Jamie's heart. It seemed something in his voice had finally cut through. Maybe not everything was lost. Maybe…

"I missed you, buddy," he said softly. He looked into Acorn's deep, dark eyes and stretched out his hand.

He didn't draw back.

Jamie touched his nose and stroked it, then slid his hand up to his forehead. "I'm sorry I let you down," he whispered. He leaned his chest against his huge head and hugged him tight. "I'm really sorry. I love you, buddy. I really do."

Acorn's skin twitched under his palms, then, slowly, the tension ebbed away from his whole body.

Oh, thank you, thank you, thank you, Jamie thought, breathless with joy.

Acorn sighed and rubbed his forehead against his chest.

Jamie pulled back and grabbed the noose around his neck. "Let's get this thing off of you!" He loosened the slipknot and slid off the longe.

Acorn shook his head and snorted with relief.

Jamie patted his forehead. "Better?"

He nudged him hard in the chest.

Jamie lost his balance and splashed into the water. Laughing, he jumped back up. "Let's go home, then!"

Acorn hesitated.

Jamie froze.

Acorn threw a glance at the woods on his left, then back at him.

A vast rift gashed through Jamie's chest. All was lost. In a second, Acorn was going to spin around and bolt away. He would never see him again. Please don't go, he thought desperately, unable to speak.

Acorn shook his head as if to wipe away something from his mind, then stared deeply into Jamie's eyes.

He felt him searching his soul, seeing much deeper than a man could ever do with human eyes. Then, without warning, he bolted forward.

Jamie's heart skipped a beat. "Yeesss!!" he roared in triumph as Acorn charged at him. He seized his mane and with a huge splash they plunged into the water.

A throb of gratitude for the generous heart of his friend shook Jamie's whole body. He held tight onto Acorn's neck as they started swimming toward the opposite shore. Right then, Jamie realized that he would remember that instant for the rest of his life: the cold rush of water on his skin; the pain in his hand; the bruise on Acorn's neck; the guilt still fresh, now receding; the bond that tied him to this creature and the sheer joy of their friendship. They were together again, he exulted, the horse and the boy...

A self-deprecating chuckle escaped his lips as he caught up with his own thoughts. "Horseboy," he mouthed.

Oh, well, his classmates got it all right, it was useless denying it. But from now on, he was going to wear their slur as a badge of honor.

The cage of pain, guilt, and misery that had kept him hostage all this time crumbled down at once. His mind cleared and his soul was clean again.

He slid onto Acorn's back as they reached the shore. Tail up, he galloped out of the water in a frenzy of sprays. Jamie pumped his fist and let out a war cry. Acorn replied with a neigh at the top of his lungs.

"Yeah, you boring people," howled Jamie at the skies. "You got that? The kings of fun are back!"

EPILOGUE

FOUR MONTHS LATER

The building of the new school stretched gray and squat against a corner of woods.

Jamie studied it, lost in thought, as students he didn't know filed in front of him and went inside. Summer had come and gone way too fast and he was now about to start a new school year in a different district.

His mom had kept her promise. Since Mr. Culvert had not wanted to help, she had bypassed him and played the trick she had hinted to: she had called the Board of Education directly. She had filed a complaint against Mr. Culvert and Ms. Ambrose. Then she had forwarded a request to transfer him to another school, citing the dire psychological toll it had taken on him. It had worked. In fact, the suited man and woman he had spotted at school the day he had defied Ms. Ambrose were not teachers, but officials of the Board of Education who had come to issue an official reprimand. That was why Ms. Ambrose had been so livid with him but at the same time had not dared to touch him.

She hadn't been afraid of him after all, he thought with some disappointment. Or maybe she had. She had certainly learned that she couldn't mess with him or his mom, and that was not too bad. She probably had never been challenged like that. He relished the idea.

What really counted was that he wasn't afraid of her anymore. He had slain the monster—literally. In fact, the same night he had confronted her, he had dreamed of a ghostly, abandoned city where a vampire hunted him relentlessly. He had been terrified of the monster, until, suddenly, he couldn't take it any longer and decided to face it. He had picked up a knife, challenged the vampire and slit its throat without hesitation, killing it almost instantly. The vampire had been a man in his dream, but as soon as he woke up, he knew it was actually Ms. Ambrose. He also realized that he had been dreaming of that place and the vampire all the time—he just forgot it every morning when he woke up. The only trace of those dreams was that dread that had stuck to him for so long. Now it was gone.

He still felt queasy thinking about how gruesome and violent the dream had been. Not to talk about the fact it didn't make any sense—killing a vampire with a knife? Seriously? Had his brain not watched enough horror movies to know better? Nevertheless, he felt there wasn't anything wrong with the dream. He felt free.

His ex-classmates instead were still stuck with Ms. Ambrose. He was hearing all about it from Sara Winters and couldn't really feel sorry for them, since they had been so vicious and cowardly with him.

He and Sara were seeing a lot more of each other these days. After she had spoken out in class to defend him, they had talked about everything and everybody and discovered they had much more in common than they first thought. He was glad to have found a new friend in her. Sara was sorry she hadn't helped him when she could have. He didn't blame her, though. He had discovered that Sara too had been bullied by the class. They had voted to make her stop raising her hand in the same way that

they had done with him. That was why Sara had been partici-
pating so little in class and had been afraid to help him. Now,
she raised her hand whenever she pleased and didn't care about
Francesca's or her classmates' demands.

Holly instead... Jamie frowned. Holly was lost—she still
hung out with Francesca. He couldn't understand what had
happened to her, to the girl that had been so happy to know
Acorn, but he knew they weren't friends anymore—for sure he
wasn't looking for her anymore.

Dan had been calling him often during the holidays. He
wanted to hang out with him, but he had kept coming up with
excuses. Probably he was being unfair, but he felt he could not
trust Dan even if he knew he was not a bad person. He was sorry,
but he much preferred the company of people like Sara or
Acorn or his mom.

He was glad he could trust his mom again. It still burned
how she had exposed him and how she hadn't defended him in
front of his father, but she had more than made up for that. Most
importantly, he knew she loved him, and even if she didn't do
everything right, he could always trust that her heart was in the
right place. Not like with his father. It hurt him that his dad
didn't like him—he wanted his affection—but he didn't want to
be abused anymore, so he steered clear of the old man.

He sighed and watched the last student sneak into the
school. He wished that things would be different in a new place,
but he doubted it. As long as he had Acorn though...

Acorn...

He turned toward home, hidden a few miles away beyond
the woods. He knew Acorn could feel him in the same way that
he could feel Acorn. He knew that probably right in that instant,
Acorn was pricking up his ears and turning his dark, wet eyes
toward him.

A ray of warmth cracked through the clouds pressing on his

chest. He was never alone. Never. Acorn was always there with him. Everything was going to be all right. He smiled.

The bell rang. It was time to go to class.

He turned back toward school. See you in a few, buddy, he thought. He took a deep breath and crossed the street.

THE AUTHOR

Lapo Melzi studied writing and filmmaking, receiving his MFA from New York University. His works have received several international award, among which is "Black Rose", now part of the permanent media collection of the Museum of Modern Art in New York. This is his debut novel.

ALSO BY LAPO MELZI

Fiction

The Last Son of the Moon

Poetry

Tree of words/Albero di Parole